Ce

WORLD HISTORY

Maya Civilization

Charles and Linda George

LUCENT BOOKS
A part of Gale, Cengage Learning

GALE
CENGAGE Learning

Detroit • New York • San Francisco • New Haven, Conn • Waterville, Maine • London

GALE
CENGAGE Learning™

LIBRARY OF CONGRESS CATALOGING-IN-PUBLICATION DATA

George, Charles, 1949-
  Maya civilization / by Charles and Linda George.
    p. cm. -- (World history)
  Includes bibliographical references and index.
  ISBN 978-1-4205-0240-4 (hardcover)
  1. Mayas--History--Juvenile literature. 2. Mayas--Social life and cus-
toms--Juvenile literature. 3. Mexico--Civilization--Juvenile literature.
  4. Central America--Civilization--Juvenile literature. I. George, Linda.
  II. Title.
    F1435.G43 2010
    305.897'42--dc22
                                                                2009053266

Lucent Books
27500 Drake Rd.
Farmington Hills, MI 48331

ISBN-13: 978-1-4205-0240-4
ISBN-10: 1-4205-0240-9

Printed in the United States of America
 2 3 4 5 6 7 14 13 12 11

Printed by Bang Printing, Brainerd, MN, 2nd Ptg., 08/2011

Contents

Foreword

Each year, on the first day of school, nearly every history teacher faces the task of explaining why his or her students should study history. Many reasons have been given. One is that lessons exist in the past from which contemporary society can benefit and learn. Another is that exploration of the past allows us to see the origins of our customs, ideas, and institutions. Concepts such as democracy, ethnic conflict, or even things as trivial as fashion or mores, have historical roots.

Reasons such as these impress few students, however. If anything, these explanations seem remote and dull to young minds. Yet history is anything but dull. And therein lies what is perhaps the most compelling reason for studying history: History is filled with great stories. The classic themes of literature and drama—love and sacrifice, hatred and revenge, injustice and betrayal, adversity and triumph—fill the pages of history books, feeding the imagination as well as any of the great works of fiction do.

The story of the Children's Crusade, for example, is one of the most tragic in history. In 1212 Crusader fever hit Europe. A call went out from the pope that all good Christians should journey to Jerusalem to drive out the hated Muslims and return the city to Christian control. Heeding the call, thousands of children made the journey. Parents bravely allowed many children to go, and entire communities were inspired by the faith of these small Crusaders. Unfortunately, many boarded ships that were captained by slave traders, who enthusiastically sold the children into slavery as soon as they arrived at their destination. Thousands died from disease, exposure, and starvation on the long march across Europe to the Mediterranean Sea. Others perished at sea.

Another story, from a modern and more familiar place, offers a soul-wrenching view of personal humiliation but also the ability to rise above it. Hatsuye Egami was one of 110,000 Japanese Americans sent to internment camps during World War II. "Since yesterday we Japanese have ceased to be human beings," he wrote in his diary. "We are numbers. We are no longer Egamis, but the number 23324. A tag with that number is on every trunk, suitcase and bag. Tags, also, on our breasts." Despite such dehumanizing treatment, most internees worked hard to control their bitterness. They created workable communities inside the camps and demonstrated again and again their loyalty as Americans.

These are but two of the many stories from history that can be found in the pages of the Lucent Books World History series. All World History titles rely on sound research and verifiable evidence, and all give students a clear sense of time, place, and chronology through maps and timelines as well as text.

All titles include a wide range of authoritative perspectives that demonstrate the complexity of historical interpretation and sharpen the reader's critical thinking skills. Formally documented quotations and annotated bibliographies enable students to locate and evaluate sources, often instantaneously via the Internet, and serve as valuable tools for further research and debate.

Finally, Lucent's World History titles present rousing good stories, featuring vivid primary source quotations drawn from unique, sometimes obscure sources such as diaries, public records, and contemporary chronicles. In this way, the voices of participants and witnesses as well as important biographers and historians bring the study of history to life. As we are caught up in the lives of others, we are reminded that we too are characters in the ongoing human saga, and we are better prepared for our own roles.

Important Dates at the Time

3114 B.C.
The earliest form of writing—cuneiform—is introduced in Sumer. In Mesoamerica the Maya calendar begins on September 8.

2560 B.C.
The Great Pyramid of Khufu is completed in Egypt.

2000 B.C.–300 A.D.
The Preclassic Period of the Maya civilization occurs during this time span.

3000 B.C.	2500 B.C.	2000 B.C.	1 A.D	250 A.D.	500 A.D.

27–c. 30 A.D.
Jesus of Nazareth performs his ministry.

300–900 A.D.
This time span represents the Maya civilization's Classic Period.

570–632 A.D.
The lifetime of Muhammad, the founder of Islam.

292 A.D.
The first evidence of the Maya Long Count is found on stelae at Tikal.

378 A.D.
Fire Is Born (Siyaj K'ak'), a warlord from Teotihuacan in central Mexico, invades Tikal.

of the Maya Civilization

600 A.D.
A volcanic eruption buries the Maya city of Cerén in modern-day El Salvador.

776 A.D.
The first recorded Olympic Games take place.

869 A.D.
The last dated monument is erected in Tikal, signaling the city's collapse.

909 A.D.
The last Long Count date is recorded on a stela in the Maya city of Tonina

750 A.D.   1000 A.D.   1250 A.D.   1500 A.D.   1750 A.D.   2000 A.D.

1300s A.D.
The Black Plague kills millions in Europe.

1847–1901 A.D.
The Caste War is fought in Yucatán.

1519 A.D.
Spaniard Hernán Cortés arrives in Mexico, thus beginning the Spanish Conquest.

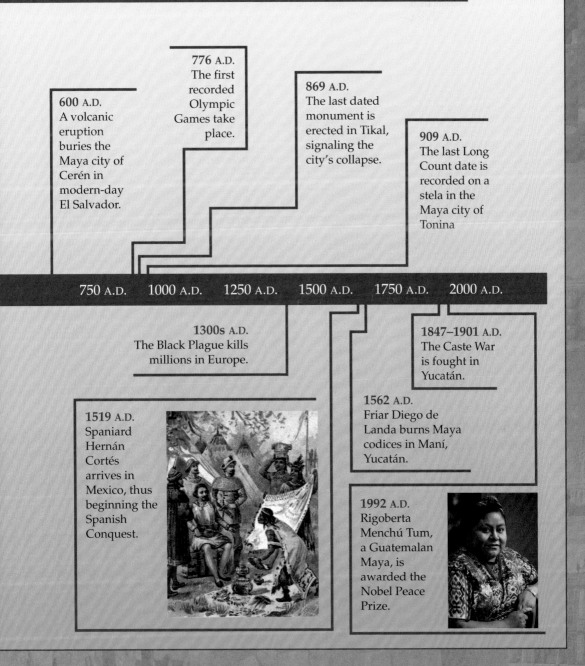

1562 A.D.
Friar Diego de Landa burns Maya codices in Maní, Yucatán.

1992 A.D.
Rigoberta Menchú Tum, a Guatemalan Maya, is awarded the Nobel Peace Prize.

The Maya: A Lost Civilization?

The Mysterious Maya. The Lost Civilization of the Maya. The Magnificent Maya. In years past each of these descriptors could have been the title of a scholarly book about this ancient Native American civilization of southern Mexico and Central America, and each would have been correctly named. Today, however, much of the mystery surrounding this pre-Columbian civilization is being revealed, and most scientists agree that the culture of the Maya is no longer "lost."

Centuries before European explorers came to the New World, the Maya were building huge cities, studying the stars, and creating a complex written language in the jungles and coastal plains of Mesoamerica—a cultural region including Mexico and parts of Central America. By the time Spanish conquistadores arrived in the 1500s, Maya cities had long been abandoned and were in a state of ruin.

Even though the classic Maya civilization no longer exists, the Maya are hardly a vanished culture. Today more than 7 million Maya people live in the Mexican states of Yucatán, Campeche, Quintana Roo, Tabasco, and Chiapas as well as in the Central American nations of Belize, Guatemala, and the western portions of Honduras and El Salvador. They are, in fact, the largest single block of Native Americans currently living in North or Central America.

Most people, however, still associate the term *Maya* with those people centuries ago who built an advanced civilization unequaled by any other native peoples of the Western Hemisphere. Evidence of that civilization—sculpture and pottery unearthed in ancient cities, an amazingly accurate calendar, and a complex system of hieroglyphic writing—has been compared with the classic civilizations of Egypt, Greece, and Rome. This highly advanced American

An artist's rendition of how the Maya city of Labna looked centuries before European explorers arrived in the New World. Archaeologists are now learning that the Maya built huge cities, studied the stars, and created a complex written language during their existence.

culture belonged to the people we call the Maya. We do not know what they called themselves. Today some Maya call themselves the Halach Winik, "the Authentic People." They speak dozens of dialects of the Mayan language—Quiché and Yucatec being the most widely spoken. Scholars use the term *Mayan* to describe only the language. For all other references to the culture, the people, or to their achievements, they use *Maya*.

Early Humans and the Land

What happened to the Maya? How did they build such a vast empire only to have it crumble into ruins? For answers, scientists have long sought information wherever they could. For more than a century scholars dug through ruined Maya cities looking for bits of pottery, burial sites, murals depicting everyday activities, and remnants of tools. Maya hieroglyphs were intriguing, but no one knew how to decode them. For scholars,

Archaeologists are learning much about Maya culture by decoding hieroglyphs that the Maya carved onto their buildings and monuments.

it was like trying to understand the Greek civilization without being able to read what the philosophers Plato, Aristotle, and Socrates, or the historian Herodotus, had written. No matter how many artifacts scientists uncovered, they could never be enough to paint a complete picture of the Maya.

Archaeological evidence tells only part of the story. Written records yield much more specific information, such as names, dates, and major events. The Maya carved many such written records onto their buildings and monuments. They also created thousands of codices—books made from rectangular pieces of bark covered with a type of plaster, tied together, and folded accordion style. Written on those "pages" was perhaps the wisdom of centuries of Maya civilization. Unfortunately, much of what Maya scribes wrote in those books no longer exists. The vast majority of the codices were destroyed at the time of the Spanish Conquest—burned to cinders in a fit of religious zeal—by priests who believed those books, and the strange markings and symbols they contained, were the work of the devil. The primary architect of that destruction was Friar Diego de Landa, who, on July 12, 1562, ordered the burning of five thousand Maya idols and dozens of codices.

Today, thanks to recent breakthroughs in decoding Maya hieroglyphs, archaeologists are finding answers to questions that have intrigued them for decades. They are learning, for example, that influence from Teotihuacan, the sprawling metropolis of more than one hundred thousand people in the valley of Mexico, helped spur the blossoming of Maya culture during the Classic Period.

Some recent discoveries have disproved earlier theories about the Maya, causing scholars to rewrite Maya history. Space-age technology—such as satellite imagery, 3-D computer mapping, and meticulous chemical soil analysis—are providing even more clues. Piece by piece the story of the ancient Maya is emerging.

Chapter One

The Rise of the Maya

No area of archaeological study has undergone a more radical change during the past few decades than the study of the ancient Maya civilization. Major discoveries seem to be made weekly at Maya sites across Mesoamerica. Other scientific investigations—primarily delving into how climate change may have affected the course of Maya history—are also shedding light on unanswered questions scientists and scholars have been posing for more than a century—about the origin, history, lifestyle, and decline of the Maya.

Breakthroughs in the decoding of Maya hieroglyphics are revealing the names of the kings and queens of individual city-states as well as dates and records of their political activities, alliances, achievements, wars, and rituals. The hieroglyphs also show the profound influence of other advanced civilizations on the Maya's development.

Since the 1960s evidence has emerged that has helped scholars gain a more thorough understanding of who the Maya actually were. According to Nikolai Grube, a professor of Maya studies in Bonn, Germany:

There are scarcely any other areas of archaeology where interpretations and ideas have changed so completely as in the field of Maya studies. . . . Although up to just a few decades ago it was still believed that the Maya had been peace-loving maize farmers who obeyed their priests' exhortations to observe the stars and honor time, it has now been proven that they were ruled over by kings and princes who were just as power-hungry and vain as potentates elsewhere in the world. . . . The extensive Preclassic cities in northern Guatemala were unknown until just a few years ago. New excavations there have caused us to date the beginning of urban civilization back by about half a millennium.[1]

Early Exploration
Early Ideas

Spanish priests and travelers during the sixteenth, seventeenth, and eighteenth centuries marveled at the ruins of gigantic pyramids they saw in Yucatán cities such as Uxmal, Tulum, Palenque, and Chichén Itzá. They wondered who had designed and constructed these amazing structures. Because of the rather primitive nature of the Maya who were still living near these ancient centers, it was thought that some other civilization must have built them. Some early visitors theorized that one of the lost tribes of Israel may have settled there. Others felt it must have been ancestors of some European or Asian culture—perhaps the Welsh, Vikings, Phoenicians, or Tartars.

Not until the 1800s did interest in Maya ruins begin to grow and be associated with the Maya themselves. In 1822 a London firm published the story of a Spanish soldier, Antonio Del Río, who had visited and excavated in the Maya city of Palenque during the late eighteenth century. His stirring account spurred further expeditions. In 1839 American diplomat, explorer, and lawyer John Lloyd Stephens (1805–1852) and British artist and architect Frederick Catherwood (1799–1854) traveled to the

Spanish explorers were amazed at the ruins of the Maya pyramids they discovered in places such as Uxmal, Mexico (pictured).

Stephens and Catherwood

John Lloyd Stephens, an American lawyer, was sent to Central America on a diplomatic mission for U.S. president Martin Van Buren. He departed for Honduras on October 3, 1839, accompanied by Frederick Catherwood. Once his diplomatic duties were completed, Stephens and Catherwood crossed into what is now Belize to explore the Maya ruins of Copán.

From Copán they made several arduous journeys to other Maya sites, visiting forty-four in all, according to Stephens, and eventually ended up at Palenque. They traveled hundreds of miles over trails bordered by volcanoes, through thick jungles, and over steep mountain ranges. They crossed rivers using precarious bridges made of tree trunks lashed together or braided lianas (vines). They slept in the ruins. While Stephens recorded their adventures, Catherwood drew exquisitely detailed images of what he saw using a camera lucida. A camera lucida used a prism to project the image of an object onto a piece of drawing paper. Catherwood later colored his lithographs with pastels.

Frederick Catherwood drew several illustrations for John Lloyd Stephens's book Voyage to the Yucatan *about the Maya ruins. This image, titled "Castle at Tulum Overtaken by Vegetation," was one that Catherwood drew while he and Stephens explored more than forty-four Maya sites.*

Yucatán and then to Guatemala. They visited various sites—some on the scrub plains of Yucatán and some deep in Central American jungles, recording their experiences in journals. Accompanying their dramatic written accounts were daguerreotypes (an early type of photograph) and intricate line drawings, graphically illustrating what they had seen.

With the publication of Stephens's *Incidents of Travel in Central America, Chiapas, and Yucatán* in 1841, interest in the Maya spread. Yet due to the remoteness of most of the ruins and their overgrown conditions—as well as the heat, insects, and snakes of the tropics—only a handful of individuals and organizations were willing to devote themselves to Maya study.

Another factor at play during the mid-1800s was the perception among most Europeans and Americans that such "civilizations" were beyond the capabilities of Native American cultures. In his 1948 book about Stephens, American archaeologist Victor Wolfgang von Hagen explains the prevailing attitude:

The acceptance of an "Indian civilization" demanded, to an American living in 1839, an entire reorientation, for to him an Indian was one of those barbaric, half-naked tepee-dwellers against whom wars were constantly waged. A rude, subhuman people who hunted with the stealth of animals, they were artisans of buffalo robes, arrowheads, and spears, and little else. Nor did one ever think of calling the other indigenous inhabitants of the continent "civilized." In the universally accepted opinion, they were like their North American counterparts—savages. No one dreamed that throughout the tablelands of Mexico, in the tangled, scrub-jungles of Yucatán, there stood, covered by jungle verdure, ruins of temples, acropolises, and stone causeways of a civilization as great in extent as Egypt's. . . . "Aztec," "Maya," "Toltec," and "Inca" were in no dictionary, and in few histories. These civilizations were not only dead, for dead implied having once lived, but, even to the world immersed in searching out the antique, absolutely unknown.[2]

Despite this culturally egocentric attitude, governments, museums, and individuals saw the opportunity to gain prestige by studying these ruins and perhaps bringing artifacts back for their national museums. Another Englishman, Alfred Percival Maudslay (1850–1931), following in the footsteps of Stephens and Catherwood, arrived in Guatemala in 1881 to begin what would become a twenty-year study of Maya ruins.

Maudslay's Pioneering Efforts

Maudslay pioneered archaeological methods that have been used for more than a century—clearing vegetation to reveal structures, measuring and drawing maps of cities, making plaster casts of carvings to be studied later, and photographing hieroglyphs to better enable their analysis. His trek began at the Maya "lost cities" of Quiriguá, located in eastern Guatemala, and Copán, located just to the south in far western Honduras. He eventually extended his study to Tikal, becoming only the second foreigner to reach that remote northern Guatemalan site.

Maudslay recorded his experiences with dry-plate photographs—an improvement over the earlier daguerreotypes—and in scientific notebooks. In his writings, however, he chose to focus not on the exciting sense of discovery he surely must have felt but rather on the hard work he saw before him. Maudslay wrote upon arriving at Quiriguá:

> Overhead and all around was a dense tropical forest; the undergrowth was so dense that we had difficulty in finding any of the monuments and even when within touch of them, so thickly were they covered with creepers, ferns and

The Compelling Nature of Maya Studies

Professor Nikolai Grube, of the Rheinische Friedrich-Wilhelms-Universität of Bonn, Germany, explains, in the introduction to Maya, Divine Kings of the Rain Forest, *why he finds the study of the Maya so compelling:*

Where else in the world are complete sites of an ancient culture hidden deep in the jungle; where else are complete regions just blank areas on the archaeological map? Where else do we know so little about the economic foundations of an ancient civilization? And where else in the world have all the great cities of a culture sunk without a trace, abandoned by their inhabitants for no apparent reason? . . .

We now have a picture of the rise and development of Maya culture that makes former representations look like rough sketches. Whereas the focus of older works focused on the exoticism of the Maya, on their differentness and uniqueness, modern publications . . . show the Maya to have been people whose problems, intentions, and motives were not so different from those of other people all over the world.

Nikolai Grube, ed., introduction to *Maya: Divine Kings of the Rain Forest.* Nordrhein-Westfalen, Germany: h.f.ullmann, 2006–2007, pp. 12–13.

moss that it was not easy to distinguish them from dead tree trunks. However, we pulled off the creepers and then scrubbed away the moss with some rough brushes we made out of the midribs of the palm leaflets and, as the sculptures began to show up, I sacrificed one of my ivory-backed hair brushes out of my dressing bag to clear out the more delicate carving of the hieroglyphics.[3]

He later wrote of the "unexpected magnificence of the monuments" of Copán; yet upon arriving at Tikal on Easter Sunday 1881, Maudslay again focused his written account on how completely overgrown the ruins appeared: "On the whole I must own to being much disappointed. The forest was over everything. The work of clearing would be much more than I could do and there appeared to be very little hope of taking satisfactory photographs."[4]

In 1881 Alfred Maudslay became only the second foreigner to explore the Maya ruins of Tikal (pictured here).

Maudslay and his porters eventually cleared much of the brush covering the central pyramids of Tikal. His photographs, published in 1902 in *Biología Centrali-Americana*, a five-volume work about his discoveries in Guatemala, provided a first look to the world at these magnificent structures. His clear photographs revealed details that Catherwood's pen-and-ink sketches and daguerreotypes could not. Scholars who were unable to make the arduous journey to Central America could now study Maudslay's photographs and learn more about Maya hieroglyphs.

Large-scale excavations and restorations, mostly funded by American universities, began about the same time as Maudslay's work but on a much grander scale. The Peabody Museum of Harvard, the University of Pennsylvania, the Carnegie Institute of Washington, Tulane University, and the Institute of Anthropology and History in Mexico each sent teams of archaeologists. Many of their projects continued well into the twentieth century, greatly adding to the world's knowledge of the mysterious Maya.

The Prehistoric Maya

Scholars have divided the chronology of Mesoamerican civilizations into specific periods of time, depending on levels of technology, architecture, and social structure. These classifications—Paleo-Indian, Archaic, Preclassic, Classic, and Postclassic—are further divided into subcategories. As new discoveries are made, however, scientists sometimes have to rethink their table of organization.

Evidence of humans—spear points, obsidian blades, residue of campfires, and shell middens (piles of trash)—has been dated to around 10,500 B.C. in caves in the highlands of Guatemala, specifically at a site called Los Tapiales. These early inhabitants lived during what scientists call the Paleo-Indian Period, extending from fourteen thousand years ago to around 7000 B.C.

During the subsequent era—the Archaic Period (7000–2000 B.C.)—groups of hunter-gatherers gradually settled in small villages. Each village probably consisted of members of an extended family and were led by the patriarch—the eldest male. These early villagers began cultivating wild plants to supplement their food supply, thus beginning the practice of agriculture. They also arranged their villages in a particular pattern that continues in use today.

Maya Settlement Patterns

A settlement pattern is how a culture lays out its settlements—how it arranges its homesteads, villages, and cities. The basic settlement pattern of the Maya was the *plazuela*, or "plaza group." It originated during the Archaic Period and developed gradually throughout the various stages of Maya history. In a *plazuela* several houses are typically placed facing each other, with a communal area in the center. This arrangement was evident in all levels of Maya society, from the Archaic Period to modern times, and from the simplest farm home to the largest city.

Arthur Demarest, a professor of anthropology at Vanderbilt University, de-

These thatched huts at Tikal, built in modern times to protect Maya stelae from the weather, may be somewhat similar to the huts and outbuildings built by the ancient Maya in their plazuela settlement groups.

scribes how the Maya eventually expanded the basic *plazuela* arrangement into larger communities:

> Usually, several houses of closely related families are placed facing each other around open courtyard living areas. In turn, several of these "plaza groups" are often placed together to form tiny hamlets of related extended families. . . . In the ancient Maya lowland sites in pre-Columbian times, such . . .

associated structures often were placed in somewhat more regular rectangular arrangements of two, three, or four platforms with huts facing each other around an open courtyard or plaza. The latter served as a living and working area for the family, as did platforms or level areas behind and near the plaza group.[5]

The same basic pattern is found in the ruins of Maya cities—with temples, palaces, and ball courts surrounding a central plaza.

A shared kitchen garden, still a common feature in rural Mexico and Guatemala, lay outside homes and other outbuildings in a typical rural *plazuela*. Chemical analysis of soil around ancient house mounds—raised earthen platforms left behind when huts that stood upon them decayed—verifies that the areas had been under cultivation. As in modern times, these kitchen gardens were used for growing plants such as squash, beans, and chili peppers to be eaten or sold at market as well as herbs for seasoning and for medicinal purposes.

The Preclassic Period

The Archaic Period was followed by the Preclassic Period, extending from 2000 B.C. to A.D. 300. Some scholars call this the Formative Period because it includes the centuries during which the Maya first began to exhibit cultural characteristics distinct from other groups. These include the rise of city-states—individual cities, ruled by a king or queen, whose power extended to the countryside and villages immediately surrounding the city. Unlike the Aztecs of central Mexico and the Incas of South America, the Maya never unified into a single empire. Instead they evolved into a less centralized feudal society. During the Preclassic Period the Maya also developed large-scale ceremonial architecture and the beginnings of hieroglyphics. The Preclassic is further divided into the Early Preclassic

Period (from 2000 to 1000 B.C.), the Middle Preclassic Period (1000 to 400 B.C.), and the Late Preclassic Period (400 B.C. to A.D. 300).

The Early Preclassic Period

The Maya of the Early Preclassic Period exhibited many distinct characteristics. Larger multifamily villages, led by a chief, were established. Agriculture was expanded to include more crops and improved farming techniques. More sophisticated art was evident in the manufacture and use of ceramics and in the development of iconographic artistic expression—the painting and carving of images of people and symbols representing ideas or events. The Maya of the Early Preclassic Period also exhibited the beginnings of a more complex, hierarchical society. During this era cultures across Mesoamerica first developed the rudiments of writing systems and an interest in measuring time and in studying astronomy.

Evidence uncovered at Cuello, an Early Preclassic site in northern Belize, indicates that these early Maya all lived in pole-and-thatch huts constructed on low earthen platforms. Archaeologists have discovered clusters of these platforms, along with artifacts left behind by their inhabitants. Evidence also shows the expanded cultivation of crops such as maize, beans, squash, and manioc.

The manufacture of ceramics is further evidence that the early Maya were settling into more permanent home bases. Particular examples of this art form have been found at Cuello as well as along Guatemala's Pacific coastal lowlands at Monte Alto, Tilapa, La Blanca, Ocós, El Mesak, and Ujuxte. At some Early Preclassic sites along the Pacific coast of the Mexican state of Chiapas—at sites such as Izapa and Ojo de Agua—ceramics and stone carvings have a marked resemblance to art from the Olmec culture that developed about the same time on the southern Gulf Coast of Mexico. These similarities indicate that the two cultures must have made contact.

A botanist uses Maya artifacts in Belize to test ancient food storage techniques. Ceramics like those pictured here are further evidence that the early Maya settled into more permanent home bases during the Early Preclassic Period.

The Olmec

The Olmec culture developed in the forested lowlands of the gulf coastal region of southeastern Mexico, southeast of present-day Veracruz. It flourished from 1200 to 400 B.C. and was long thought to have been the *madre cultura*, or "mother culture," of Mesoamerica. The Olmec people were thought to have created the first cities, the first monumental structures, and a remarkably accurate calendar; they also developed a particular type of ball game that became a common feature of many Mesoamerican cultures. Recent discoveries along the Pacific coast of southern Mexico and Guatemala, however, have been tentatively classified as early Maya and may prove to have been built as early as, or perhaps before, anything built by the Olmec.

The Middle Preclassic Period

During the Middle Preclassic Period, from 1000 to 400 B.C., a more hierarchical class structure continued to develop. The old tribal society became more similar to the feudal society of medieval Europe or the city-states of ancient Greece, with leadership in the hands of a single king or queen and an elite upper class to support that ruler. Members of the developing Maya upper class were either religious, military, or political leaders. Such leaders usually demanded the construction of public structures. Many of these structures were used for governmental or religious ceremonies, but others were monuments and ornate tombs to honor the leaders themselves. Examples of such public architecture can be seen in the Pacific coastal lowlands of Guatemala, at Abaj Takalik and Cocola, as well as at Kaminaljuyú, in that nation's central highlands.

During the final centuries of the Middle Preclassic Period, the Maya spread farther inland from the Pacific coastal areas. During these years they established ceremonial centers at Piedras Negras, Seibal, Cival, Dos Pilas, and El Perú, expanding steadily toward the north and east. They carried with them the trend toward larger ceremonial centers and more extensive public architecture.

Archaeologists have discovered two of the largest ceremonial centers ever built by the Maya at Nakbe and El Mirador in the Petén region of northern Guatemala. El Mirador, for example, features two of the largest Maya pyramids—La Danta and El Tigre—which compare in size with the Great Pyramid in Egypt. Archaeologists believe these structures were used as raised platforms for religious ceremonies. No tombs have been discovered beneath them.

The Late Preclassic Period

In the Late Preclassic Period, from 400 B.C. to about A.D. 300, the Maya further developed their writing system, their calendar, their interest in astronomy, and their level of artistic expression. These intellectual developments are demonstrated in temples with stuccoed and painted facades, such as those found at El Mirador, and in dramatic murals such as those discovered at San Bartolo in extreme northeastern Guatemala.

The Late Preclassic is the period of Maya history that has undergone the most rethinking due to recent discoveries in the jungles of northern Guatemala and the coastal regions of Guatemala and El Salvador. These discoveries have proven that the Maya civilization of the Late Preclassic Period already displayed characteristics, beliefs, and practices that formerly were only associated with the Classic Period.

The Classic Period

Over the next six centuries—from A.D. 300 to 900—the Maya enjoyed their golden age during the Classic Period. Maya city-states evolved from purely ceremonial centers into full cities surrounding the ceremonial centers, some with populations in the tens of thousands. Each was ruled by a succession of single kings or queens, with a much more organized nobility to support the ruler and oversee the day-to-day operations of the city-state. Evidence is also emerging that some of the kings of Maya city-states during the Classic Period may have been outsiders—nobles from Teotihuacan, for example. During the Classic Period, the Maya civilization reached its peak of population and the pinnacle of its intellectual achievement, yet it never unified into a centralized empire.

Each Maya city-state featured a huge, ornately decorated ceremonial center with steep-sided pyramids topped with temples and palaces. Many of these pyramids were built atop the richly decorated tombs of their rulers and were continually being rebuilt, layer upon layer. Beyond the ceremonial center were outlying structures that housed artisans, craftsmen, and bureaucrats. Farther out, and in the surrounding countryside, were farmers and laborers who supported the elite. Most of these city-states were located in the Petén region of northern Guatemala and in the southern Yucatán lowlands.

The Maya civilization of the Classic Period shared characteristics that originated during earlier periods of Maya history. These included an interest in astronomy, the recording of the passage of time in a calendar, artistic expression, a system of writing, and the construction of public monuments. All of these came together in the stone stela, an architectural feature that set apart the Maya cities that were built during this period. A stela is a stone column erected in a public location to commemorate a particular event or person—usually the birth, marriage, accession to the throne, military

A common architectural feature found in Maya cities during the Classic Period is the stela, which was often erected to commemorate a particular event or person. This stela depicts a Maya king in full regalia.

victory, or death of a king or queen. Classic Maya cities have many stelae, whereas cities constructed earlier—during the Preclassic Period—do not.

Maya stelae are almost the only remaining written record of Classic Maya history. Because so many of the civilization's books, or codices, that had recorded historical events were lost to the fires of fanatic Spanish priests, the stelae are virtually all that are left to tell that history. Likewise, the carvings on the surfaces of many stelae have eroded away over the centuries, making those that survive even more precious.

Each stela featured the face of a mythological figure or an actual ruler on one side, with hieroglyphic carvings of dates, names, and events on the other. They were erected in central areas, in front of temples and palaces, so the public could view them. The earliest dated stela sits in the central plaza of Tikal, with the equivalent of the date A.D. 292 carved onto its side. The latest stands at Tonina, in southern Mexico, and is dated A.D. 909.

Deciphering the stelae that dot the central areas of Classic Maya cities has revealed specific information about those cities and the leaders who ruled them. They provide clues about the relations between individual Maya city-states, including their alliances and wars. The stelae have also helped fill gaps in scholars' understanding of Maya society during the Classic Period. One particular stela—Tikal's Stela 31—has now been decoded and validates a long-held theory. The stela provides written evidence that an invasion by an outside force significantly altered the development of Classic Maya civilization.

The Arrival of Fire Is Born

According to the hieroglyphic record of Stela 31, the invasion occurred on January 8, 378. A large, well-armed force dispatched from the mighty city of Teotihuacan in central Mexico and arrived at the Maya city of Waka (now called El Perú) in present-day northern Guatemala. At the head of this invading army was a warlord named Siyaj K'ak'—"Fire Is Born." Dressed in extravagant feathered headdresses and carrying javelins and mirrored shields, Fire Is Born's army impressed the local ruler, Sun-faced Jaguar. Sun-faced Jaguar welcomed the envoy into his city and formed an alliance between his city and Teotihuacan.

Fire Is Born's ultimate goal, however, according to Stela 31, was the conquest of Tikal, a major Maya city-state some 50 miles (80km) to the east. His mission, it seems, was to bring the region of north-central Guatemala under Teotihuacan's control, either through persuasion or force. To that end, he recruited additional warriors from Waka and marched on to Tikal less than a week later. After defeating that city's army on January 16, his forces killed Tikal's king, Chak Tok Ich'aak—Great Jaguar Paw—and destroyed most of that city's stone stelae, replacing them with their own, celebrating their victory. According to Stela 31, which was erected a generation later, Fire Is Born was proclaimed "Lord of the West," and later presided over the enthronement of a new foreign ruler, perhaps a son of the ruler of Teotihuacan, Spear-thrower Owl.

Until the arrival of Fire Is Born, the Maya remained politically fragmented, each city-state charting its own path. After A.D. 378 Maya culture blossomed, alliances were formed between city-states, and great advances in science and technology took place. According to author Guy Gugliotta in an article for *National Geographic*:

> Though fragmentary, the evidence that has emerged over the past decade suggests that this mysteri-

ous outsider remade the political leadership of the Maya world. Mixing diplomacy and force, he forged alliances, installed new dynasties, and spread the influence of the distant city-state he represented, the great metropolis of Teotihuacan near present-day Mexico City.[6]

Over the following decades Fire Is Born's name appeared on monuments all across the Maya's territory. In his wake the Maya of the Classic Period achieved a level of civilization unsurpassed in the Americas that endured for more than five hundred years.

Chapter Two

Maya Nobility of the Classic Period

The Classic Period of Maya history ended centuries before the arrival of the Spanish. Therefore, most of what scholars know today about the upper classes of Maya society comes from archaeological evidence found in their cities. This evidence includes the tombs of Maya kings, the carved records of the stelae, and detailed images and hieroglyphs on ceramic vessels and murals. In the ruins of the Maya city of Bonampak, located in the western edge of the Mexican state of Chiapas, ornate murals inside the tomb of a Maya king paint a vivid picture of life at court during the Classic Period. These include detailed images of how the nobility of Classic Maya city-states looked—what physical features and adornments they considered stylish.

In these images Maya society is portrayed as having strict social classes, with a king and queen at the top; priests, nobles, warriors, and artisans slightly lower in rank; and common people below that. Some Maya kings ruled over only the city-state in which they lived. Others, through alliances, outside influence, intermarriages, and conquest, created dynasties that controlled several city-states from a central location.

Maya society had two classes of people: the elite and the commoners. The elite were called *ah mehenob*, or "higher men," in Yucatec, a Mayan language in use at the time of the Spanish Conquest that is still spoken in the region. Commoners were called *yalba uinicob*, or "lower men." The *ah mehenob* were further divided into subclasses. The ruling class—kings and queens—though few in number, occupied the highest level of society. According to hieroglyphs, the highest rank in Maya society was the *ahau*, or "lord" (sometimes spelled *ajaw*). This title was used by the ruler and others within the nobility. Beginning in the fourth century A.D., however,

Maya rulers referred to themselves as *k'uhal ahau*, or "divine lord." After the arrival of Fire Is Born in A.D. 378, rulers in the Petén region included the term *kaloomte* in their titles—"Lord of the West"—emulating that conqueror's title and emphasizing their connection with Teotihuacan.

The Lifestyles of Maya Royal Families

The king and queen of a Maya city-state were revered as gods. As such, they were not expected to work like common people. They spent their time presiding over elite councils, making decisions that affected their city-state. They lived in lavish palaces within the city state's ceremonial center, attended by numerous servants. According to murals found in many Classic Maya cities, each king wore a feathered headdress, a cape made from the brilliantly colored feathers of quetzal birds, intricate jade and shell jewelry, and sometimes an elaborate mask to make him appear godlike.

Much is known about Maya kings and queens because hundreds of carved stelae commemorate their achievements and still stand in the central plazas of Classic Maya ceremonial centers. The Maya called these multiton stone monuments *lakamtuun*, or "big/banner stones" and erected them whenever anything happened of historical note. In their book *Chronicle of Maya Kings and Queens*, Nikolai Grube and Simon Martin describe what was usually carved on stelae: "Carved with the king's im-

Archaeologists know quite a bit about Maya kings and queens because of the hundreds of carved stelae that still stand, as well as other carvings, like this one, that commemorate their achievements.

age, often shown standing on a bound captive or iconic location, their inscriptions go on to chronicle the major historical events that have occurred since the last stone was set up."[7]

Scholars often can read the stelae, murals, and pottery and know when members of the nobility were born, who their parents were, where they came from, whom they married, what they achieved during their lifetimes, and how and where they were buried. Most kings and queens were buried in elaborate

The King's Headdress

Nikolai Grube, a professor of Maya studies, explains the significance of the headdresses worn by Maya kings:

Although the king's clothing differed from that of the commoners and the nobility in lavishness and the number of attributes, it was the headdress that distinguished him from all others. There were several different kinds of headdresses, but all contained the long, green-gold tail feathers of the quetzal bird. . . . They formed the basis for masks of gods and animals and other objects of the greatest symbolic value that were intended to express that the wearer was under the protection of the gods. . . .

Because they were believed to have a soul, the headdress and other attributes of power [of a king who had died] had to be looked after and cared for like living things; in particular, they had to be provided with nourishment in the form of offerings such as blood and incense.

Nikolai Grube, ed., *Maya: Divine Kings of the Rain Forest.* Nordrhein-Westfalen, Germany: h.f.ullmann, 2006–2007, pp. 96–97.

Although Maya kings wore several different kinds of headdresses, all of them contained long, green-gold tail feathers of the quetzal bird. This image, carved on the wall of a Maya tomb, shows a typical headdress.

tombs that featured colorful murals depicting their lives. Because much of Maya hieroglyphic writing has been translated, these individuals now have names and life stories.

Royal succession was primarily patrilineal, meaning it followed the ancestral line on the father's side. As is often the case in kingdoms, eldest sons usually became heirs to their father's throne. Princes were called *ch'ok*, meaning "noble youth," and the heir apparent was called *b'aah ch'ok*, the "head youth." Queens did rule some Maya city-states of the Classic Period, but only when no male heir could become king and the dynasty might otherwise have fallen.

Communicating with the Gods

Scholars know that Maya kings and queens, once in power, had their lives virtually dictated by the rituals demanded by the complex Maya calendar. Their primary duty was to conduct public religious ceremonies—either alone or serving alongside priests—as mediators between their people and the gods. During those ceremonies they performed ritual dances or participated in a particular ball game. They also sought visions—messages from the heavens.

Archaeologists believe the Mesoamerican ball game may have originated as early as the fifth century B.C. and that its popularity spread as far as the modern-day southwestern United States. Stone ball courts are present in virtually every Maya city. Most courts are I-shaped, with a long, narrow playing field flanked by sloped or vertical walls, often with stone rings placed high on the opposing walls. The game, played in some ways like soccer, was a key element of the Maya creation story. Maya kings regularly played the game to reenact the adventures of the mythical figures called the Hero Twins, whose actions were believed to be essential to pave the way for the creation of humanity as well as to establish the relationship between the gods and humans.

Part of that relationship was communicating with their gods, and only rulers were considered worthy to receive such messages. To induce the trances they believed were necessary to receive these visions, Maya kings and queens put themselves through ordeals of pain and deprivation—going without food or sleep, smoking tobacco, and inflicting wounds on themselves to allow their blood to flow. Blood, the essence of life, was sacred to the Maya, and royal blood was considered the ultimate offering to the gods. In addition to providing a blood sacrifice, the blood loss weakened the individual and helped induce the trancelike state necessary for a vision quest.

During public ceremonies Maya kings drained blood from their earlobes, tongues, and genitalia using stingray spines, bone needles, or obsidian spikes. Queens are depicted pulling barbed cords through their tongues. In both cases royal blood dripped onto paper strips, which then were burned. It

A figure of a Maya nobleman on display at a museum. Nobles served as priests, scribes, diplomats, engineers, local administrators, and government bureaucrats.

was believed that smoke from the bloody paper mingled with smoke from incense burners and rose to feed the gods.

Priests

Some archaeologists believe religious ceremonies were performed exclusively by Maya kings and queens. Others, however, believe that a group of specially trained people—priests—must have performed those duties. No archaeological evidence proves conclusively that a separate class of nobles existed that served as priests during the Classic Period, but some believe it must have because a powerful Maya priesthood existed at the time of the Spanish Conquest. These scholars insist it is logical to assume that such a specialty also existed earlier in Maya history.

At the time of the conquest, the high priest in each city-state, the *Ahaucan May*, was the keeper of the calendar and the sacred chronicles—records of Maya history and astrological charts. The priest's knowledge of astronomy and mathematics allowed him to predict events such as the arrival of comets and eclipses of the sun or moon. They were also responsible for teaching and passing on the history of their people, including knowledge of Maya hieroglyphic writing.

Below the high priests were assistants—the *ahkinob*, or "they of the sun"—who conducted most day-to-day tasks. The *ahkinob* kept temple fires burning, made sure incense burners stayed lit, and made daily offerings to the gods. These lower priests also were responsible for advising those who came to consult a priest about astrological matters—what day would be best for a wedding or what to name a child, for example. Priests lived in or near the temples and wore ornate robes and sometimes masks and headdresses.

Other Nobles

Beneath the upper *ahau* class were other nobles, many of whom served as government bureaucrats, trade representatives, diplomats, local administrators, or engineers—those who designed and supervised the building of temples, palaces, causeways, irrigation systems, and other public structures. The members of this level of Maya nobility were wealthy landowners called *uytzam chinamital*. They shared the easy lifestyle of the king. Their homes—fine stone buildings with roofs of stone—were clustered near ceremonial centers. They, too, wore fine robes and jewelry, and many were buried in decorated tombs.

Another important member of Classic Maya nobility was the *aj tz'ib*, the scribe ("he, the writer, who draws"). Unlike the priest, who recorded historical events hieroglyphically, the scribe's role was more closely related to that of an accountant, keeping track of taxes and tributes and making sure everyone paid what they owed the king. Commoners were required to pay taxes (usually food, cloth, feathers, or other items of value), and representatives from conquered lands were required to pay tribute to the king with valuable items such as jade, obsidian, feathers, or cacao beans. Martin and Grube explain the importance of scribes—comparing their list of expected tribute with what was actually presented to the king—as portrayed in murals and on painted ceramics:

Tribute scenes show the king seated on a sumptuous throne covered with jaguar skin. Vassals kneel before him holding out bundles of fine materials, feathers and bags of cacao beans. . . . [The aj tz'ib] compared the goods being handed over with their list of tributes. Such scenes give a rare insight into the economics of the Maya states and show that one of the king's most important activities was that of increasing his personal wealth as well as that of the society as a whole.[8]

Images of Beauty

For the Maya nobility, public displays of wealth and physical ornamentation

Initiation Ceremonies for Young Maya Nobles

In their book Chronicle of the Maya Kings and Queens, *Simon Martin and Nikolai Grube describe how a young heir had to prove his worth:*

Childhood was marked by a series of initiation rites, one of the more important being a bloodletting usually performed at the age of five or six. . . . Although [their lineage] was their main claim to legitimacy, [older] candidates still had to prove themselves in war. A bout of captive-taking often preceded elevation to office. . . .

Kingly investitures [ceremonies celebrating the crowning of a new king] were elaborate affairs made up of a series of separate acts. There was an enthronement, the heir's seating on a cushion of jaguar skin, sometimes atop an elevated scaffold bedecked with celestial symbolism and accompanied by human sacrifice. A scarf bearing a jade image of *huunal*, the "Jester God" . . . an ancient patron of royal authority, would be tied to his forehead. An elaborate headdress of jade and shell mosaic, trailing green iridescent plumes of the quetzal bird, would follow. . . . The name carried in childhood was now joined by *k'uhul k'aba'* "divine name," usually taken from a predecessor, sometimes a grandparent.

Simon Martin and Nikolai Grube, Chronicle of the Maya Kings and Queens: Deciphering the Dynasties of the Ancient Maya. London: Thames & Hudson, 2000, p. 14.

A Maya artisan with tattoos on his shoulder and legs records events on a stela. Tattooing and body painting were quite common among both Maya men and women, and people without such markings were often looked down upon.

demonstrated their status. Hairstyles, clothing, jewelry, tattoos, and intentional scars were part of their public image. One of the most visible demon-strations was how they styled their hair. In ancient times Mayan noblemen wore their hair long, either braided around the head with a pigtail hanging down the back, carefully braided in ornate designs across the scalp, or arranged into an intricate design atop the head. If they had a pigtail, it almost always had an obsidian disc hanging from its tip. At times, a man might cut the hair on top of his head short, or singe it off, as part of the overall design. Facial hair was discouraged, and many pulled it out with copper tweezers. Women's hairstyles could be quite elaborate. They formed their hair into sculptural designs—mostly on top of their heads—and fixed it in place with tree sap, honey, or other substances that dried in place. Some women's hairstyles stood more than 1 foot (.3m) above their heads.

The practices of tattooing, intentional scarring, and body painting were quite common among both men and women of the Maya elite classes, and the colors and designs employed by individuals were indications of social position. Tattoo designs were pricked into the skin with a sharp bone, and pigment was then rubbed into the wounds. This was an extremely painful experience, so tattoos represented valor and courage. For intentional scarring, the goal was a raised scar in a particular pattern. To accomplish this, the skin was cut or pierced in the desired pattern. Then, to make sure substantial scars would form, the individual encouraged the growth of the scars by keeping the wounds open for a time. Any adult without tattoos and scarring patterns was looked down upon.

Michael D. Coe, a professor emeritus of anthropology at Yale University, discusses body ornamentation in his book *The Maya*. According to Coe, the Classic Maya thought certain physical adornments enhanced their appearance or publicly identified them with a particular social class:

> Both sexes had their frontal teeth filed in various patterns, and we have many ancient Maya skulls in which the incisors have been inlaid with small plaques of jade. Until marriage, young men painted themselves black (and so did warriors at all times); tattooing and decorative scarification began after wedlock, both men and women being richly elaborated from the waist up by these means.[9]

The colors used for body and face painting were very important to Maya men. Young unmarried warriors and men who were fasting painted themselves black. Blue was the color of priests and the color that victims of sacrificial rites were painted. Women usually painted their faces red.

A feature unique to the Maya was a dramatically sloping forehead, but this was not a natural characteristic. It had to be shaped very early in life in order to form the head into what the Maya felt was a noble appearance. Coe describes the procedure:

> Immediately after birth, Yucatecan mothers washed their infants and then fastened them to a cradle,

Jade: The Green Gold of the Maya

Few materials are as durable as jade. In Mesoamerica it was prized above all other stones. Jade is green, and to the Maya it symbolized the color of sprouting maize. Maya artisans carved it into jewelry for the nobility, but commoners also decorated themselves with necklaces of small jade beads that they passed on from generation to generation.

Jade is a collective term for several types of green or blue stones, including albite, chrysopras, serpentine, and a combination of jadeite and diopside. All jade processed in Mesoamerica originated in the valley of the Rio Motagua in southern Guatemala. It was found as loose rocks and stones, ranging in size from gravel to rocks weighing several hundred pounds. Cutting jade was relatively simple. First, a sharp obsidian blade was used to score the rock. Then rope, a flat piece of hardwood, or a piece of slate was moved back and forth—with sand, crushed obsidian, or jade dust acting as an abrasive—to slowly cut halfway through the rock. The jade was then turned over, and the procedure was repeated. When only a thin section remained, a sharp blow completed the cutting.

This jade necklace and beads were excavated from a Maya king's grave in Takalik Abaj, Guatemala. In the Maya culture both the nobility and commoners decorated themselves with jade jewelry.

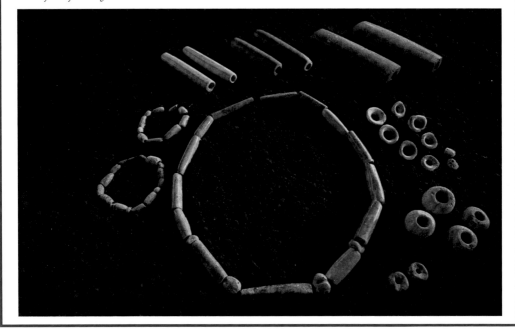

their little heads compressed between two boards in such a way that after two days a permanent fore-and-aft flattening had taken place which the Maya considered a mark of beauty.[10]

Another practice, usually employed at the same time, was an attempt to cross the child's eyes. This was also considered a mark of beauty and distinction among Maya upper classes. Many of the Maya gods appear with crossed eyes. Parents hung a nodule of resin or a small bead from the middle of their child's forehead—the child would naturally focus on the bead, thus crossing its eyes.

Jewelry, too, was a widespread adornment for Maya nobles, both men and women. Most highly valued was jade; it was green—the color of plants and thus a symbolic color of rebirth—and it was rare. According to archaeologist Charles Gallenkamp, "Older children had their earlobes, septums [tissue that separates the nostrils], lips, and one nostril pierced so they could wear a variety of ornaments."[11] Such piercings were usually performed on the children of the elite when they reached the age of five or six.

Two of the most common forms of jewelry, at least among the upper classes, were jade choker necklaces and ear pendants, both worn by men. The necklaces usually featured a pectoral, a larger piece of carved jade made into the necklace and displayed on the up-per chest. This emblem signified his family's status and lineage. These necklaces were either passed from father to son or were included in the items buried with a person of great rank. Ear pendants were inserted through the earlobes, with progressively larger and larger inserts, and usually made up of several pieces of ornately carved jade.

In all cultures certain physical features and adornments are considered desirable and others are not. In cultures with distinct social classes, a person's appearance is often an indication of status, wealth, and position. Maya ruling elite of the Classic Period reflected that trend. They wore large amounts of jade, quetzal feathers, and obsidian—all relatively rare and expensive items.

Outward appearance was the most visible difference between Maya nobility and the common class. Even though Maya commoners used many of the same techniques to achieve what they believed to be beautiful, they could not afford to go to the extremes of the upper classes. Whereas nobles led lives of ease due to extravagant wealth and power, commoners had to work—on the farms, in the quarries, in the workshops, and in the markets. Their simpler lifestyles required simpler clothing, more utilitarian hairstyles, and jewelry and other physical adornments that were less expensive. Although less adorned than the upper class, the commoners were the backbone of the Classic Maya civilization.

Chapter Three

Commoners of the Classic Period

During the height of the Classic Period, scholars estimate that as many as 20 million Maya lived in Mesoamerica. They believe that up to 98 percent of that population must have been commoners, and the majority of commoners were farmers. Without the labor and support of such a large underclass, the Maya nobility could never have achieved such a high level of civilization. However, the lower classes—those who cleared the land, grew the crops, and quarried the stone—were seldom represented in Maya art. Few artifacts have been found belonging to common people, other than stone and bone tools, bits of utilitarian pottery, grinding stones, and the earthen mounds that indicate the former locations of peasant huts.

For that reason scholars have a severely limited knowledge of Maya commoners during the Classic Period. Many of their theories about the lower classes have been based on the writings of Spaniards such as Friar Diego de Landa. These Spaniards observed first-hand how the Maya lived at the time of the Spanish Conquest and during the Colonial Period (1521–1810). Likewise, scholars have also observed how rural Maya peasants live today in Mexico and Central America.

The *Yalba Uinicob,* or "Lower Men"

According to de Landa and others who wrote about the Maya during and after the Spanish Conquest, two classes of commoners—*yalba uinicob*—lived in Classic Maya society. The upper level of commoners was made up of skilled artisans and merchants—what might today be considered a middle class; the lower level consisted of unskilled laborers. Skilled artisans and craftsmen included stone and wood carvers, stucco workers, painters, potters, and

In Maya society, an artisan such as this one who produced pottery would have been considered a member of the upper level of commoners.

sculptors. These individuals produced the monuments, murals, and ceramics that had been designed and engineered by members of the *ahau* class. Traders and lower-level bureaucrats were also part of this Maya "middle class."

Merchants and tradesmen—almost always men—bought and sold the goods each city-state produced. They also traveled from place to place, trading with their city-state's neighbors—sometimes hundreds of miles away. Their homes were usually stone, but they were smaller, less ornate, and located farther from the city's center than those of the *ahau* class.

Lower-level commoners were unskilled workers. In rural areas this included primarily farmers, but in urban areas they were stonecutters, cleaners, and porters. Farmers wore simple cotton garments and sandals, and they raised food for themselves and to support the king, the royal family, and the nobility. All land was considered the property of the king, as in most feudal societies. During the dry season, many farmers provided labor for the construction of causeways, temples, and palaces. They also cut wood for fuel and timber, but scholars agree it was the food they produced on their farms that was the key to the Maya civilization's success in the region's harsh climate.

Peasant Houses

Most commoners lived on the outskirts of cities or in the jungle. Their homes were simple huts constructed of poles, mud, and plaster with steeply pitched roofs thatched with palm fronds. Most Maya houses were oval, round, or rectangular, and they were constructed using a wattle-and-daub technique. A row of poles was set in the earth, and mud was packed in between the poles, thus creating thick, solid walls when the mud dried. Inside a typical Maya house, the space was divided into two sections by a tall partition. The front served for everyday activities, and the rear for sleeping. Other smaller structures often stood near the house, serving as kitchen or storage areas. The entire complex was built atop a low earthen platform to ensure adequate drainage.

Because of their simple construction, peasant houses lasted only one generation before being torn down. Each time the resident of a house was buried in the earthen platform on which the house had been standing, and a new house was built on the raised platform. The Maya believed that this practice kept the spirits of their ancestors nearby.

A commoner's home had very little furniture. Cooking was done on a stone hearth, usually with ceramic vessels. Other kitchen equipment consisted of woven baskets and bags, clay pots, hollowed-out gourd scoops, stone implements, and perhaps wooden chests. Every kitchen also had a metate and a mano—stones specifically used for grinding maize. Stools and benches, constructed by tightly lashing together wooden poles and covering the framework with woven matting, served as seating. Low beds were constructed in much the same way, with woven matting stretched across lashed poles.

Archaeologists can learn a great deal about a family's social standing during the Classic Period by excavating and studying the family's home. Professor Arthur Demarest explains how the location, design, and contents of excavated huts can help scholars understand Maya social classes:

Some of the social patterns of Classic Maya society were "fossilized" in architecture and artifacts in the ruins of household groups. For each household group the amount of stone masonry (versus mud and thatch) often varied with the social rank of the ancient inhabitants. Height and area of household platforms, the presence or absence of monuments, distance from the nearest epicenter, the number of courtyards, presence of plastered floors, and the types of pottery and artifacts in burials are all clues to the social and political standing of a group's ancient inhabitants.[12]

The New World's Pompeii

In 1976 a Salvadoran bulldozer operator accidentally bumped into the buried remains of a wall belonging to an ancient Maya house. He notified authorities, work was halted, and two years later, when excavations began, archaeologists discovered an almost intact farming village from the Maya Classic Period. They believe the village was buried under 9 to 18 feet (3 to 5m) of ash when a nearby volcano erupted, probably around A.D. 600. The site, called Cerén, is located in the Zapotitán Valley, 20 miles (32km) northwest of El Salvador's capital city, San Salvador. Cerén is providing archaeologists their first peek at a rural Maya village as it existed during that time.

Nicknamed "the Pompeii of the New World," Cerén is being carefully excavated by a team of archaeologists from the University of Colorado, Boulder. What they have found in the village and the surrounding farmland challenges some of what scholars have theorized about rural peasant life during the Classic Period. The area was apparently covered with volcanic ash fairly rapidly, preserving it just as the eruption of Mount Vesuvius preserved the ancient Roman cities of Pompeii and Herculaneum.

Scientists have not unearthed any human remains at Cerén, leading them to assume the population had enough time to flee before their village was buried. Huts have been uncovered that still have the occupants' straw bedding tucked into the rafters—just as modern Maya peasants do, to store their bedding out of the way during the day—indicating the disaster probably occurred in daytime. Among the discoveries made at Cerén are clues to how the Maya villagers farmed their land and what crops they grew—to feed the Maya.

The Maya village of Cerén, nicknamed "the Pompeii of the New World," was well preserved due to being buried with ash when a nearby volcano erupted. Findings during excavation of the site is challenging many theories archaeologists have about Maya civilization during the Classic Period.

Feeding the Maya

One of the biggest mysteries surrounding the Maya of the Classic Period, until recently, has been how Maya farmers were able to wrest enough food from the relatively poor soils of the Yucatán and the highlands of Guatemala to support a population large enough to have built such massive cities. Studying food production and consumption is often the cornerstone of understanding ancient cultures, and apparently Maya farmers excelled at maximizing their food production, even under extremely difficult growing conditions.

Although kings and nobles no doubt ate more lavishly, even Maya commoners consumed a balanced diet. For years, scientists thought corn, or maize, made up more than 50 percent of the daily food intake of the Classic Maya—that it alone provided the bulk of their nutrition. It is true that maize was a significant food source, as well as a central element in Maya mythology and frequently a prominent feature of their monumental art. However, scientists have long doubted the Maya could have grown enough maize to feed the populations that are now being attributed to Maya cities of that period—often with a population density that would compare with that of the suburbs of a large modern American city. Around Tikal, for example, scientists estimate an urban population density during the Classic Period of about 300 people per square mile (115 people per sq km). That is roughly equivalent to the population density of Nashville, Tennessee, according to the 2000 census.

Recent discoveries at Cerén seem to indicate that another plant—manioc root—may have been just as important to the Maya diet. Payson Sheets, leader of the group excavating Cerén, believes that what they are finding may change scholars' ideas about which foods kept Classic Maya society going for so long. They found evidence of some corn cultivation below the thick layer of volcanic ash, but they are also finding row upon row of once-flourishing manioc plants.

Manioc, a common root crop in the American tropics today, is a hardy plant that produces a waxy, relatively tasteless root. Its flesh can be made into anything from tortillas to liquor. It is easy to grow, thrives virtually anywhere, packs loads of carbohydrates, and provides about six times the calories of an equivalent amount of corn. It is usually boiled and eaten like a potato. It can be grated, fried, turned into flour, or, when sugar is added, made into a dessert. It has long been known that the Maya ate manioc, but it was thought to have been a minor part of their diet. This is largely because, as a root crop, evidence of its cultivation during ancient times is virtually impos-

sible to find. Seeds like corn might survive centuries under the proper conditions, but not roots.

At Cerén, however, Sheet's team has excavated fields where manioc was grown—meticulously weeded, and in long, straight, parallel rows to maximize production. The manioc roots themselves are gone, of course, but thanks to the protection of the volcanic ash, cavities in the ground that remained after the roots shriveled away are mostly intact, similar to the cavities that remained after the bodies of those who perished and were buried in Pompeii disintegrated. Excavators carefully filled the manioc cavities with plaster. Once the plaster hardened and was dug up, they produced almost perfect casts of manioc roots.

According to Sheets, "We're seeing what they actually grew, as they grew it. In other places you might get bits of pollen, small pieces of evidence. Here you see the techniques, the furrows, the farm implements, everything."[13] Although their discoveries have been encouraging, Sheets is quick to point out that finding evidence in a small peripheral Classic Maya location like Cerén does not prove that the cultivation of manioc took place across all of Maya territory.

Maize and Other Foods

Despite the implications of the discovery in El Salvador, corn was, and is still, a mainstay of the Maya diet. Besides the ever-present tortilla, the Maya used cornmeal in almost everything they ate

Maya Farming Practices

Maya farmers of the Classic Period used the slash-and-burn, or swidden, method of farming. Underbrush on a particular plot, or *milpa* (a word borrowed from the Aztecs that means "field"), was chopped down with a stone ax, or *bat*, leaving the larger trees for shade and to hold the soil. Eventually—usually in the dry season of late March, April, and May—the then-dry debris was burned, leaving cleared land with a rich layer of carbon and ash to serve as fertilizer on which to plant seeds.

Planting was done by Maya farmers—then, as now—with a simple, fire-hardened digging stick called a *xul*. Heavy rains in June and July germinated and sustained the crops, with a minimum of weeding, until harvest. This method, however—which is still used in much of the world—tends to deplete the soil after only a few years. More land then must be cleared and planted while the original field is allowed to lie unplanted, or fallow, for some years to rebuild its fertility.

A stone ax probably used by Maya farmers during the Classic Period.

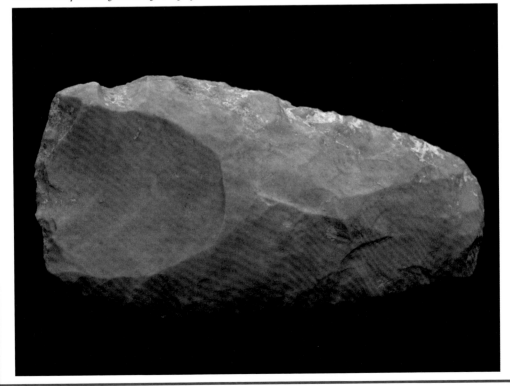

or drank. With corn and possibly manioc to provide the carbohydrate—a source of energy—they ate beans for protein, and squash and chili peppers for essential vitamins. Add to that a few fresh fruits and an occasional bit of meat, and they consumed everything their bodies needed.

Besides their staple foods, the Maya also grew sweet potatoes, tomatoes, avocados, jícama, papaya, mulberries, melons, and pumpkins. The squash-like fruit of the chayote, a vine that grows all across the Yucatán Peninsula, was also a favorite. Two fruit trees in particular have been associated with Classic Maya sites, so much so that in some cases finding them helps explorers locate remote structures that have been completely covered by jungle. The first is the breadnut or ramon tree (*Brosimum alicastrum*), which produces an edible nut enclosed in an edible fruit capsule. The fruit, an important source of protein, was valued by the ancient Maya also because the leaves could be fed to their domesticated animals.

The other tree found quite often around Maya sites is the amapolla tree (*Pseudobombax elipticum*), prized in part, according to Professor Peter D. Harrison, because it "bears bright red fruit, with no leaves visible. Not only was red a sacred color to the Maya, the color of the East and of the rising sun, which they worshipped as a god, but it came to represent the color of life— possibly because of the association with blood." However, the main reason the Maya valued the amapolla was because its sap, which they could easily collect, could be "fermented to make a highly intoxicating drink."[14]

For meat, the Classic Maya fished and hunted small game such as deer, rabbits, armadillos, as well as tapirs. Birds, turtles, and iguanas also made their way into the Maya stew pot. They captured red deer and peccaries, which they held for short periods in pens prior to slaughter. They raised domesticated turkeys, ducks, bees, and dogs. Their dogs were used in hunting, but were also fattened to be slaughtered and eaten.

The Maya were skilled beekeepers. They cultivated bees and housed them near their homes in hollow logs sealed at each end with mud. In addition to using honey as a sweetener, they mixed it with tree bark and fermented it into a popular drink called *balche*.

Besides *balche*, the Maya also loved to consume cacao, usually in the form of a relatively bitter drink mixed with ground corn. The Maya cultivated cacao trees (*Theobroma cacao*) on the Pacific coast, on the western Yucatán Peninsula north of Belize, and in the lowlands of the Mexican state of Tabasco beginning in the Middle Preclassic Period. The trees are fairly delicate, and can grow only under specific climatic conditions. Cacao blooms are pollinated exclusively by mosquitoes, so they thrive in the shade of larger trees. Because of their scarcity, cacao beans were highly prized, and traded as far away as central Mexico during the Classic Period, and used as currency during the Postclassic Period.

Hot Chocolate

In Mesoamerica the Maya—commoners and nobility alike—enjoyed a bitter beverage made from cacao beans. Nobles may have had it often, but commoners considered it a luxury because of the scarcity of the beans. The hot chocolate people drink today is usually made with milk and sugar, but neither was used during the time of the Maya. Instead they mixed cacao with chilies, making a spicy, bitter drink. Sometimes they mixed it with ground maize or flavored it with a cinnamon-like bark called canela.

Family Life

Daily life for Maya commoners was controlled by forces they could neither see nor understand. The Maya believed in astrology—that the position of the stars, movement of the planets, and phases of the moon had power over them, and that priests could interpret the celestial signs for them. In the world of the Classic Maya, common people left it to priests to determine the correct person for them to marry, the best days to get married, when to have children, and what to name them. The birth of a child was a significant event in a Maya family, and each date foretold the person's attributes—some good, some neutral, and some bad.

A child's given name (first name), or *paal kaba*, was carefully chosen during a ceremony conducted by a lower priest. Each child was given four different names—his *paal kaba*, his father's family name, his mother's family name (or *naal kaba*), and finally an informal nick-name, or *coco kaba*. Masculine given names began with the prefix *Ah*, and feminine given names began with *Ix*. Some examples of these given names might have been Ix Cuy ("Owl"), Ah Tok ("Flint Knife"), and Ah Kukum ("Jaguar").

About the age of four, girls were given a red shell—a symbol of virginity—to be worn on a string tied around their waists until puberty; boys, in turn, had a small white bead fastened to their hair. No evidence has been found of formal schools among Maya commoners, but boys and girls learned what they needed to know from their parents. When boys reached the age of fourteen and girls the age of twelve, they went through a coming-of-age ceremony, were considered old enough for marriage, and could leave home.

All Maya marriages were arranged, either by a child's father or by an *ah atanzahob*, a professional matchmaker. After the marriage, the groom lived

A Maya woman weaves a mat. Weaving was just one of the domestic chores that Maya women performed on a daily basis.

with and worked for the bride's family for six or seven years. At that time, he could build a separate home for his family near his own parents' house.

Women took care of domestic chores such as collecting firewood, gathering and preparing foods, weaving cloth for clothing, and making household containers from clay, gourds, and other materials. Leisure time was almost nonexistent, but most families attended public religious ceremonies. Many of these events involved music, with instruments such as drums, flutes, bells, and trumpets. They also might watch dramatic presentations, with actors presenting stories from their mythology.

Maya children older than four or five had little leisure time. As soon as they were old enough, they joined their parents and put work ahead of play. When they had some free time, children played a board game with beans that was similar to Parcheesi, or they played with balls made from the elastic gum of rubber trees. Boys ran and chased each other, playing the hunter and the hunted.

The stories of the lives of common people—those upon whose backs the Maya civilization was built—vanished almost as soon as they died. Scholars are fortunate to have the accounts of Friar Diego de Landa and others describing in

Calling the "Doctor"

When a Maya commoner fell ill, the women of the family usually knew folk remedies or herbal cures to try. However, if the illness persisted or was beyond the skill of the local practitioner, a priest might have to be called. After examining the victim, the priest might prescribe such treatments as rituals, fetishes, or potions. These potions might consist of such everyday ingredients as herbs, plants, or minerals, but they could also contain such unsavory elements as bat wings, animal excrement, blood, urine, bird fat, red worms, or crocodile testicles.

A typical remedy, translated from a Maya source, gave instructions for deadening the gums before extracting a tooth:

There is an iguana that is yellow beneath the throat. Pierce its mouth, tie it up and burn it alive on a flat plane until it is reduced to ashes. These ashes of the iguana you are to anoint [apply to the gums]. . . . Then you shall draw the tooth without pain. Try it first on a dog's tooth, before you draw the man's tooth.

Quoted in Charles Gallenkamp, *Maya: The Riddle and Rediscovery of a Lost Civilization*. New York: Viking Penguin, 1985, p. 126.

detail the homes, appearance, clothing, food, and activities of the common Maya at the time of the Spanish Conquest, but they can only infer from those sources what life was like for the Maya during the Classic Period.

They are fortunate, too, that the Maya village of Cerén is being unearthed, revealing more details about commoners of the Classic Period. These sources, along with the ruins of Maya cities, undisturbed Maya tombs, what remains of the codices prepared by Maya scribes, and hieroglyphs carved onto stone monuments, help scholars better understand the Maya of the Classic Period—who they were and what they achieved during their golden age.

Chapter Four

Greatest Achievements

The most visible achievements of the ancient Maya are their vast cities and towering pyramids. Advances in architectural design and building techniques helped them create cities and monuments that rivaled those of ancient Mesopotamia, Egypt, Greece, and Rome. Upon closer inspection, though, more subtle inventions and discoveries come to light—discoveries that allowed the Maya civilization to develop to a level that enabled it to design and construct those enduring structures.

Agricultural Practices

Increases in Maya population during the Late Preclassic and Classic periods made it necessary to clear more land and increase production. The Maya built extensive irrigation systems and developed other intensive agricultural practices, such as the construction of terraces on hillsides and raised beds in swampy areas. The practice of terracing made thousands of acres of otherwise unproductive land available to Maya farmers. Terraces of various types—some built during the Classic Period—are still in use today by Guatemalan and Mexican farmers.

As much as 30 percent of the Yucatán consists of damp, swampy areas called *bajos*—lowlands—that are unsuitable for normal farming practices. In the Petén region in the central lowlands of Guatemala, that portion rises to 50 percent, with only drier upland areas suitable for *milpas*. To reclaim swampland for farming, the Maya built raised beds for crops. They constructed a checkerboard-like pattern of these raised beds in the *bajos* by scooping mud from the bottom of channels and piling it up between them.

The roughly rectangular artificial islands they created were then used for raising crops. Because the soil was constantly refertilized every time they added more of the organically rich mud, farmers were able to grow some crops year-round, greatly increasing food production. Without such intensive agricultural practices, it would have been impossible to provide enough food to support the population required to construct the Maya's most visible achievement—stone cities.

Stone for the Pyramids

Cities built by the Maya in the Late Preclassic, Classic, and Postclassic periods reflect superior intellect and craftsmanship. The city-state of Tikal, for example, may have covered 47 square miles (122 sq. km) during its heyday, with a "downtown" area of some 6 square miles (16 sq. km), roughly the size of the National Mall in Washington, D.C. Towering over Tikal's central Great Plaza are numerous stone pyramids—tombs of their kings— and on either side rise two massive stone pyramid-temples, Temple I and Temple II. Like most Maya pyramids, these were built using limestone quarried nearby.

Limestone is relatively soft and easy to cut into blocks while still in the ground. It hardens after being exposed to air. During the Late Preclassic Period the Maya discovered that they could cut grooves into the natural limestone rock with flint or obsidian tools, deepen the grooves, and eventually use levers and wedges to separate a stone block.

Then, while the limestone block was still damp, they carved it roughly into the shape they needed using wooden hammers or hammer stones and stone chisels. Workers used a wooden sled to transport the block to the building site, where craftsmen finished carving and polishing it. If the limestone was particularly soft, as it was near Palenque, craftsmen used a special twin-bladed stone knife to complete the carving.

Urban Architectural Developments

Pyramids like those at Tikal and Palenque, along with hundreds of others in cities such as Piedras Negras, Quiriguá, and Copán, reflect two advancements in architecture and building techniques similar in some ways to those of the Roman Empire—the arch and cement. The Maya developed the use of arches in their construction, but theirs were not true arches, like those built by the Romans. Instead the Maya built corbelled arches for many of their doorways and as high ceilings for many of their pyramids' rooms. A corbelled arch is formed when stones forming layers, or courses, on opposite walls are extended gradually toward the center of the open space. Each course sticks farther out into the space until the opposite walls meet, forming a triangularly shaped ceiling with a capstone on top, connecting the sides. Because this type of arch cannot span much open space without collapsing, rooms topped with them had to be somewhat narrow.

Like arches, Maya cement also differed in some ways from what the Romans used. Yet it served the same purposes: mortar to affix stone to stone in a wall, and stucco to seal the surfaces

These pyramids at Tikal show how the Maya used cement to meet their own unique structural and architectural needs.

of structures and decorate their walls with raised images and hieroglyphs. The Maya burned limestone, pulverized it, and mixed it into a substance similar to cement. The mixture formed a bond so tight that stones joined with it seemed to be naturally joined—as if the structures were made of one piece of stone. During the Middle and Later Preclassic periods, the Maya used stucco to adorn the walls and steps of their buildings, usually with three-dimensional images from their mythology.

Pyramids

All Maya pyramids share certain characteristics. They are step pyramids rather than smooth-sided "true" pyramids like the Great Pyramid of Egypt, and all are topped by other structures. Maya pyramids, in general, have three components: a stepped pyramidal base with a stairway leading to the top, a chambered sanctuary or temple atop the pyramid, and an ornamental masonry "topknot"—called a roof comb—stretching skyward from the roof of the temple. Though they serve no practical purpose, these roof combs give Classic Maya pyramids their distinctive look. Scholars believe they were added to Classic Period pyramids to increase their height and make them appear more imposing, more sacred, and closer to the heavens.

At the northern Guatemalan Classic site of Tikal—"City of Echoes" in Mayan—sit six large pyramids with roof combs. So impressed was filmmaker George Lucas with Tikal that he used its skyline as a backdrop for several scenes in the 1977 movie *Star Wars*. Pyramids at Palenque, a Maya site in the Mexican state of Chiapas, all have

unique roof combs. Instead of the solid roof combs of Tikal, each Palenque structure is topped with a latticed roof comb, ornately carved with scenes from Maya mythology.

Known Maya pyramids number in the thousands. They make up the majority of structures in the central areas of Maya cities. Whereas some served as tombs, others were foundations for temples, astronomical observatories, or other government buildings. Thanks to hieroglyphic carvings on the structures, archaeologists usually are able to determine when each was built and by whom. What archaeologists do not know is how many more Maya pyra-

Some Mayan temples, such as this one at Copán, are known as "stacked" pyramids because they have been built on top of older pyramids. This stacking preserves the carvings and structure of the older buildings.

mids remain undiscovered in the dense jungles of the Yucatán Peninsula and Central American highlands, mistaken for tree- and vine-covered hills.

Some Maya pyramids are buried beneath other pyramids that were built at a later date. It was common practice among Maya kings in the Classic Period to build a larger pyramid over one built by a predecessor, often using the older structure as the foundation for the new one. In some cases the pyramids are stacked one inside the other. For example, Temple 26 in Copán, Honduras, sits atop at least six previously built pyramids. Scholars can literally dig their way through the history of the city and its kings.

Often these "stacked" pyramids each contain a king's tomb, allowing excavators to see how each dynasty differed from those that preceded it. Many of the covered structures were carefully preserved in the process, protecting them from the elements. As each layer of the newer pyramid was laid in place, workers carefully packed sand between the new structure and the old, covering the carvings on the older pyramid to form a solid core for the new structure. Archaeologists tunnel into pyramids, remove the sand, and study the carvings and hieroglyphs on older pyramids.

Across the region, some two hundred Maya centers have already been found, most containing numerous pyramids. Whereas some are in well-known ceremonial centers, such as Tikal, Copán, Uxmal, Palenque, and Chichén Itzá, others are in lesser-known, more recently discovered sites. Some Maya pyramids are simple platforms on which temples were built; others are steep, ornate structures with many levels. Many contain tombs, such as the Pyramid of the Inscriptions at Palenque and Temple I at Tikal, but others do not.

Some pyramids were used as foundations for astronomical observatories. The Caracol at Chichén Itzá in the northern Yucatán is one example of this. This structure is one of the few round Maya structures and was built atop a step pyramid to elevate it above the surrounding terrain for observation of the rising and setting of the sun, the moon, the planet Venus, and other heavenly bodies. The Caracol, which means "Snail" in Spanish, was named for its internal spiral staircase, which resembles the pattern on a snail's shell.

Paintings and carvings on temple walls, along the facades of pyramids and other structures, on countless pieces of ceramic pottery, and on stelae depict scenes of life in every Maya city. Alongside these paintings and sculptures are thousands of smaller carvings that early archaeologists recognized as a form of hieroglyphic writing. For centuries no one knew what the Maya had written, but today they do.

Maya Hieroglyphics

Other civilizations in the New World recorded their history, mythology, and sometimes their business transactions, but the Maya were the only ones in the Western Hemisphere to develop a complete, complex system of writing. It was

As this monument shows, the Mayan language is a mixed language containing both pictograms and syllabograms. Most Maya hieroglyphs can be read by scholars now, and this allows researchers to learn more details about the Maya culture than was possible before.

to convey the word *snake*, the Maya drew a small snake, usually stylized within a roughly square image. Had their written language used only pictograms and number symbols, they could have recorded rudimentary stories about events that occurred around them, but if they had wanted to write *air*, for example, or *beauty*, pictograms would have been far too limiting.

To enrich their written language, the Maya developed symbols called ideograms to represent nonphysical concepts. They had symbols for concepts such as love, hate, anger, and pride. The use of ideograms allowed them more freedom of expression, but they also wanted to express the phonetic sounds of their spoken language. They therefore developed symbols called syllabograms to represent sounds. Each syllabogram contained one consonant and one vowel; like English, a vowel could be pronounced more than one way, so the Maya devised different syllabograms for each pronunciation.

Because of its use of pictograms (also called logograms—"word signs") and syllabograms, Maya writing is referred to as a logosyllabic language, or a mixed system. About eight hundred writing signs have been identified so far, and most can now be read, allowing scholars to understand minute details about the Maya—names, places, and concepts—they could not read before.

Maya hieroglyphic texts are read from top to bottom, left to right, two glyphs at a time. As scholar Heather McKillop explains, "To read a glyphic

so complex that fifty years ago no scholar could read it. Now the subtleties of the Maya's written language are gradually coming to light.

Like the ancient Egyptians, the Maya incorporated pictograms into their system of writing. A pictogram is a picture that represents an object. For example, text on a Classic stela, for example, one begins at the top left corner, reads the first two glyphs, and then continues reading glyphs below them, by pairs. Once at the bottom, one returns to the top of the text and reads the next column of glyphs, again by pairs."[15]

Today scholars can read most of what they find in Maya cities, revolutionizing the study of this ancient civilization. According to scholar Michael D. Coe:

The history of the American continent does not begin with Christopher Columbus, or even with Leif the Lucky, but with those Maya scribes in the Central American jungles who first began to record the deeds of their rulers some two thousand years ago. Of all the peoples of the pre-Columbian New World, only the ancient Maya had a complete script: they could write down anything they wanted to, in their own language. In the last century, following the discovery of the ruined Maya cities, almost none of these records could be read by Western scholars. . . . Today, thanks to some remarkable advances made by epigraphers [those who decipher hieroglyphics] on both sides of the Atlantic, we can now read most of what those long-dead scribes carved into their stone monuments. I believe that this decipherment is one of the most exciting intellectual adventures of our age, on a par with the exploration of space and the discovery of the genetic code.[16]

One of those epigraphers, the late Linda Schele of the University of Texas, said, "These glyphs give the Maya 1,500 years of history, written in the words of their ancestors, not in the words of white people from Europe."[17] Simon Martin, another epigrapher and the coauthor of several books on the Maya, adds, "This is our one and only opportunity to peer into the Americas before the arrival of Europeans and hear these people speaking to us. . . . [It gives] us an indigenous insight into what they thought was important."[18]

One thing "they thought was important" was the study of astronomy. Much of what the Maya wrote—on stelae, ceramic pottery, and temple walls—involved what they observed and predicted, based on studying the stars.

Keeping Their Eyes on the Heavens

In cities throughout the Yucatán, alongside pyramids, ball courts, and temples, the Maya built observatories to watch the skies. The Maya gods resided in the heavens, so worship included watching the sky. Centuries of watching the sun, moon, and stars rise above the horizon eventually led the Maya to develop a sophisticated astronomy. Early scholars noticed that the location from which the heavenly bodies emerged on the horizon varied depending on the season. They studied the phenomenon by driving two stakes in the ground or by placing two vertical stones to align them with the location on the horizon of those celestial events. Over time they noticed recurring

Tourists visit the ruins of the Caracol, a Maya observatory, at Chichén Itzá. Observatories allowed the Maya to predict celestial events with much greater accuracy.

patterns that made it possible for them to predict when certain events would occur. They eventually built stone observatories with windows aligned with those points; this allowed them greater accuracy in their predictions.

During the Late Preclassic and Classic periods, they built pyramids and plazas along astronomical lines. They aligned these structures with the path of the sun on certain days of the year or with the cardinal directions. At many of these pyramids, a person standing at the entrance of the temple could look out over the surrounding smaller pyramids and perhaps see the sun rise directly over one pyramid on the summer solstice, over another on both the fall and spring equinoxes, and over yet another on the winter solstice.

Some sites, however, did not align their structures with the path of the sun. Instead they aligned them with the paths of other celestial bodies. One example is at Takalik Abaj ("Standing Stones"), a Late Preclassic site near the Pacific coast of western Guatemala. Scholars believe its builders aligned the structures with the star Eta Draconis in the serpent-shaped constellation Draco. Scholars speculate that the city may have been the center of a cult that worshipped that star or the god they believed it represented.

Without the use of telescopes or computers, Maya astronomers achieved a remarkable degree of accuracy. They were able to chart the movement of stars and planets—calculating, for example, that the revolution of the planet

Venus, what the Maya called Chak ek', took 584 days. Modern astronomers know that its revolution is precisely 583.92 days, a margin of error just over one-hundredth of 1 percent. Using only fixed lines of sight, crossed sticks, and fixed observation points, Maya astronomers and mathematicians also calculated the length of a year on Earth to be 365.2420 days, incredibly close to the actual figure of 365.2422. They were also able to predict the changing of seasons, the arrival of comets, and the occurrences of solar and lunar eclipses.

Mathematics and an Obsession with Time

The Maya's intense study of astronomy required the simultaneous development of an equally complex system of mathematics. Theirs was vigesimal—based on the number twenty—rather than decimal, based on ten. They also developed the concept of zero, possibly as early as 36 B.C. Although it seems basic to modern cultures, zero is a relatively complicated mathematical idea. It was unknown in Europe until the Middle Ages, when the idea finally found its way from India, by way of the Arabian Peninsula. No symbol for zero appears in Roman numerals because the Romans did not consider it necessary to have a numeral to represent nothing. Advanced mathematics would be useless without it. Without zeros, how could numbers less than one— 0.003, for example—be written?

Both fields of knowledge, astronomy and mathematics, were essential for the

Maya's true obsession—time. No ancient civilization, in the Old World or the New, was more obsessed with the passage of time than the Maya. Mathematics and astronomy were tools for the creation of the most important technological advance for the Maya—their calendar. Almost twelve hundred years before the adoption of the Gregorian calendar that most of the world uses today, the more accurate Maya calendar was in use.

The Maya became obsessed with their calendar as part of their religious observances. The Maya's numerous gods and goddesses lived in the heavens and embodied certain stars, moons, and planets. Therefore, studying and anticipating the repeating cycles of these celestial bodies became an important impetus to develop and maintain a calendar. The Maya believed that the passage of time controlled the universe. Alexander W. Voss, a professor at the University of Quintana Roo in Mexico, explains why the Maya calendar was so closely associated with their gods: "In a never-ending cycle [the gods] were born, developed their powers and then died, only to be born again at a precisely determined time and start a new cycle. To the Maya, these supernatural entities represented time and were responsible for maintaining cosmic order."[19]

Because these cycles were thought to be crucial to their survival, observing certain religious ceremonies on certain days of the year was also thought to be crucial. Using their calendar each day, the *aj k'inob*, literally, "lords of the day," predicted important events and calculated which supernatural being, good or evil, would rule that day. They then performed ceremonies they felt would best influence the cosmic entity in their favor.

The Maya Calendar

Maya scribes listed dates on almost every painting, stela, and ceramic vase they created, but they never seem to have carved or otherwise depicted their entire complex calendar. Some sources suggest that the circular stone calendar of the Aztecs—sometimes referred to as the Aztec Sun Stone—also represented the Maya calendar, but the two are totally different. The Maya calendar was actually three separate calendars that ran at the same time, and no graphical depiction of all three has been discovered.

The secular Haab calendar, based on the solar year, contained eighteen sections, each having twenty days, which constituted one *Tun*. At the end of each *Tun* was a separate period of 5 days to finish the 365-day year. This 5-day period, called *u wayeb u haab*, "sleepers of the year," or *ma k'aba k'in*, "the nameless days," was considered unlucky. Each *Tun* in the Haab calendar begins with the Maya month Pop and ends with Kumk'u, which is then followed by the Wayeb, the empty, unlucky days. The days of Haab began with 1 Pop, 2 Pop, 3 Pop, and so forth, and they ended with 3 Wayeb, 4 Wayeb, and 5 Wayeb.

Longer time periods in the Haab had different terms. A *K'atun*, for example, was a period containing 7,200 days, or twenty *Tuns*. Their largest measure-

A Unique Maya Pyramid

El Castillo, the pyramid that dominates Chichén Itzá, is not dedicated to a god of Maya origin. It is dedicated instead to Kukulcán, the Maya name for the feathered serpent god the Aztecs called Quetzalcoatl. It is also unlike any other Maya pyramid. El Castillo is an almost perfectly symmetrical square pyramid with stepped sides. Although it has a large temple at its peak, it lacks a roof comb, and staircases ascend all four sides of the pyramid. El Castillo more closely resembles something the Aztecs or the Toltecs would have built, suggesting that perhaps the Late Classic Maya were influenced by those central Mexico cultures.

Before the excavation site was sealed to preserve it, visitors could enter an opening beside the north stairway, climb the steps of an earlier pyramid upon which El

Castillo was built, and see Kukulcán's throne, all inside the current pyramid! The throne has the form of a snarling red jaguar, with jade eyes and spots and shell fangs. Standing before the throne is a sculpture called a chacmool, a reclining figure holding a plate over its belly, probably to hold a sacrificed human heart.

An Aztec painting of Quetzalcoatl, the feathered serpent god known to the Maya as Kukulcán, to whom the pyramid El Castillo *is dedicated.*

This modern artist's creation, produced for sale to tourists, combines elements from the Aztec calendar with the Haab, the Maya solar calendar. The hieroglyphs in the inner circle are Maya glyphs for months, but the outer rings come directly from the Aztec Sun Stone. The ancient Maya never carved a stone version of their calendar, and these elements would never have appeared together on any authentic Maya artifact, stelae, or building.

ment of time was a *Bak'tun*. This was a period of 144,000 days, or 20 *K'atuns*—approximately 394 years. *Bak'tuns* were used to describe dates in the far distant past or future. The Maya felt the end of a *Bak'tun* was a particularly significant date because of their belief in the im-

portance of observing cycles. The custom of observing the changing of one century to another—as happened at the beginning of the twenty-first century—is a modern example of humankind's ongoing fascination with repeating cycles of time.

The Tzolk'in was the Maya's ritual calendar of 260 days. Each day of the Tzolk'in had a name consisting of two parts—a number and a day symbol. There were 20 recurring day symbols, but the numbers 1 through 13 were used. As the ritual year progressed, numbers and day symbols followed a set pattern until they reached a total of 260 days. At that point they repeated, beginning a new cycle. Each cycle of the Tzolk'in began with 1 Imix, 2 Ik', 3 Ak'bal, 4 K'an, 5 Chikchan, and so on.

Although the nonreligious Haab and the religious Tzolk'in ran independently of each other, the Maya combined them into a larger cycle of 18,980 days—52 years—that has been called the Calendar Round. Any particular Haab day—such as 9 Kumk'u—would not coincide with a particular Tzolk'in day—5 Imix, for example—more than once every 18,980 days. At the end of those long cycles, every 52 years, the Maya feared the end of the world. Priests performed special religious ceremonies they felt would prevent that from happening.

The Classic Maya also developed what scientists call the Long Count, which was a way to measure even longer periods of time, extending back to a specific date. This compares with the Christian practice of recording time in Anno Domini (A.D.)—years since the birth of Jesus Christ—or, more recently, years of the Common Era (C.E.). The date that was considered the beginning of Maya time, and hence the beginning of the Long Count, has been calculated to have been September 8, 3114 B.C.—the day on which they believed the current world was created. The Maya believe time extends backward and forward into infinity. Some carved stelae mention dates some 400 million years in the past.

In addition to the Haab, the Tzolk'in, and the Long Count, the Maya studied lunar cycles to predict lunar and solar eclipses. They also were obsessed with the planet Venus—Chak ek', or "Great Star," which they associated with war. Professor Voss explains that the Maya considered Venus "a bringer of misfortune, bad omens, and war,"[20] so they had a calendar to predict its position in the sky. Many extensive battles between city-states, the deaths of kings, and the fall of dynasties took place during the rising of the planet Venus.

To the Maya, time ran in cycles; whatever happened in a particular year, or time of year, was bound to happen again. During the empty days —the Wayeb—people were careful to avoid anything that might cause them harm because they were convinced it would happen repeatedly. If someone tripped and fell on an empty day, they expected to continue tripping and falling every day for the rest of their lives.

The ancient Maya did not see time as merely a means of arranging events in order. Time had mystical significance. In their minds, a different god ruled over each period of time, and they had to know which god to worship at the appropriate time. To put it in our terms,

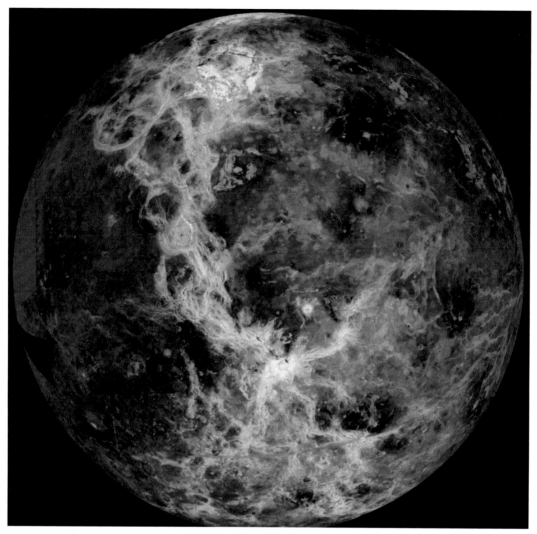

The Maya seemed obsessed with the planet Venus, which they associated with war and misfortune.

the god of January would rule until midnight on the 31st, when the god of February would take over. Because not all Maya gods were benevolent toward humanity, some time periods were more dangerous than others.

Everything the Classic Maya accomplished related to their religion. They built pyramids to get closer to the heavens. They created a calendar and studied the stars to better know how to worship their gods. They played a ball game to imitate the actions of their gods. Even the food they raised was linked to the gods. To the Maya, their lives—and their universe—were like

The Mesoamerican Ball Game

The Mesoamerican ball game, played in specially constructed courts in virtually every Maya city throughout their history, was possibly the foundation for the modern games of football, soccer, basketball, volleyball, and other ball games. Based on fragmentary evidence, scholars believe it was played as either a team sport or an individual competition by both men and women. Players wore protective clothing, including headgear, knee pads, and quilted cotton armor. Some were depicted wearing what the Spanish called a *yugo*, which was a yokelike, heavy wooden shield in the shape of a horseshoe that was worn around the stomach.

The ball—varying in size up to 12 inches (30cm) in diameter—was made from latex obtained from local rubber trees. It was relatively hard and could weigh as much as 18 pounds (8kg). Once the ball was tossed into play, it was allowable to hit it back and forth only with the hips, thighs, or upper arms. The ultimate goal was to put the ball through a ring. Maya kings often played the game to symbolically reenact scenes from the Maya creation myth.

A model depicts a Maya ball game being played. This game may have laid the foundation for the games of football, soccer, basketball, volleyball, and other ball games.

2012—The End of the World?

The end of the thirteenth *Bak'tun* is approaching on December 21 or 23, 2012. Some believe this to be the end of the Maya Long Count, when the Maya supposedly predicted the end of the universe; but Maya scholars dispute this. They say it will simply be the end of one time period and the beginning of another—similar to the end of one calendar year, when December 31 again becomes January 1. Based on stelae at Copán, they believe the true end of the Maya Long Count will not occur for trillions of years. Some have compared what will happen on December 21 or 23, 2012, to an odometer in an older car. When it has exceeded its mechanical limit, it simply turns over to all zeros and starts the count again.

Popular fiction and Hollywood blockbuster movies are playing up these erroneous doomsday predictions. One movie, *2012*, starring John Cusack, was released in November 2009. Its trailer alludes to the Maya prophecy, ominously saying, "We were warned!"

the maize plants that fed them: They sprouted with new life, grew to maturity, bore fruit, then withered and died. But the seeds of those plants, when cared for properly, could be placed in the Earth, nurtured, and would sprout again, thus perpetuating the cycle of birth, life, death, and rebirth. The calendar told the Maya to which of their many gods and goddesses they should pray on a particular day, make offerings, and, in some cases, make blood sacrifices to ensure the continuation of that cycle.

Chapter Five

The Spirit Realm

Just as everyday life for the ancient Maya was influenced by their calendar—such as when to plant and harvest crops or when to attend public ceremonies—so were their religious beliefs and practices. The Maya believed time was an integral part of how the cosmos functioned. It was crucial for their religious ceremonies to be appropriately timed. Their calendar—and its associated mythology—was a window to the distant past and to the future. It gave the Maya a connection to the previous universe and the evils that led to its destruction, to the creation of this current universe, to its eventual destruction, and to the creation of the next universe.

The Maya Universe

The Maya had an elaborate view of the heavens, Earth, and Xibalba—what they called the underworld—and how events were interconnected in each level of the universe. They believed the heavens were divided into thirteen levels, each with a specific god ruling over it. They believed Xibalba, the "Place of Fright," contained nine levels; each of those levels was presided over by a different, often grotesque, deity. The Maya did not conceive of the underworld as necessarily a place where immoral or evil people went when they died. It was where all people went, except those who died a violent death. All who went to Xibalba had to face tricky challenges from the gods of the underworld. If a soul was successful in outwitting those gods, it ultimately ascended into the sky as a heavenly body.

Only those who met a violent death would enter some level of Heaven. These souls went to the level of Heaven presided over by the god who ruled the element of nature that led to their deaths. A person who was struck by lightning or drowned, for example, went to the level ruled by Chaak, the god of rain, thunder, and lightning. War casualties and sacrificial victims inhabited the level reigned over by K'inich Ajaw, the god of war and blood sacrifice.

Gods in the heavens and in the underworld controlled what happened on Earth, including rain, the seasons, and sunrises. Kings and priests performed ceremonies and blood sacrifices to nurture the gods and strengthen them for those tasks. This belief in the interconnectedness of the universe, seen and unseen, affected not only the Maya's daily lives but also how they built their homes, laid out their *milpas*, and constructed their cities. The orientation and design of buildings and plazas and the construction of main roads and causeways reflected this obsession with imitating on Earth the order and structure they perceived in the universe.

The Maya conceived of Earth as a flat square. Each of its four sides faced a cardinal direction, and each had its own color—red for east, white for north, black for west, yellow for south, and bluish green at the center. Earth was held up at each corner by four ancient gods, above the primordial ocean from which it rose at the moment of creation. The corners of Earth were the points at which the sun rose and set on the summer and winter solstices. At the center of each side lay a mythical mountain with a cave. These were entrances to Xibalba and the primordial ocean. The water above which Earth floated was a link with the underworld. Another Maya source shows Earth resting on the back of a monstrous crocodile, floating in a pond of water lilies.

A statue of Chaak, the god of rain, thunder, and lightning found at the Maya ruins of Copán. According to the Maya religion, people who were drowned or struck by lightning went to the level of heaven ruled by Chaak.

The Maya believed that honoring the cardinal directions was paramount, that mountains connected Earth to the heavens, and that caves and cenotes—natural sacred wells—linked Earth to the primordial ocean below. Pyramids simulated mountains, and temple doorways represented caves—symbolic entrances to the underworld. Entering a cave or a temple doorway was symbolic of direct contact with the gods. Many major temple complexes in the lowlands of Yucatán were built directly over caves, and sacrificial altars have been discovered in many caves in the region.

Many cities in the Yucatán were also built near deep circular-shaped cenotes, into which sacrifices to the gods were often thrown. Friar Landa reported that, in times of drought, the Yucatán Maya threw people into the cenote near Chichén Itzá. When confronted about killing people in this way, they insisted that the individuals who had been cast in were not dead, even though they were never seen again. The Maya believed that those sacrificial victims had simply entered the underworld through the cenote and were still alive there.

In the Maya universe the sky was supported by either another set of four gods or four huge trees, depending on the source consulted. In the center, serving as an axis to connect the upper world (the heavens), the middle world (Earth), and the underworld, stood a huge ceiba tree—the World Tree. In some representations this center of the universe was a stalk of maize rather than a tree. (The ceiba, or silk-cotton tree, is the tallest tree in the Maya region of Mesoamerica, reaching a height of 230 feet [70m]. Called *yaxche* ("first tree") in Mayan, they are sacred and are never cut down when farmers clear land for planting.)

A stylized image of the World Tree was carved on the rear wall of the sanctuary in the Temple of the Cross at Palenque. The temple was named for the cross-shaped World Tree in the bas-relief carving; the tree is pictured growing out of a sacrificial bowl with the great bird of heaven—Itzam Ye—sitting at its highest point. Itzam Ye was one symbolic form of the Maya's supreme deity, the creator god Itzamnaaj.

The Creation Myth

The core of the Maya religion—and the primary reason behind their rituals—was their creation story. The Maya believed humans were created to serve and nurture the gods, and they acted accordingly. During virtually every religious ceremony, Maya kings and queens symbolically reenacted the creation story, reinforcing that belief in their subjects.

The Maya creation story must be gleaned from several sources. Inscriptions in three temples in Palenque, including the one in the Temple of the Cross, provide many details. Similar inscriptions have been found in temples in Quiriguá, Piedras Negras, Cobá, and Copán. Accounts are also found in the *Popol Vuh (The Council Book* or *The Book of Counsel)*, a sixteenth-century Maya text that retells their ancient creation story, and in *The Books of Chilam Balam (Books of the Jaguar Prophet)*, a series of twelve books written by Maya village priests after the Spanish Conquest.

According to these sources, the world as it exists today was created on the

The Maya creation story must be gleaned from several sources, including this page from the Popol Vuh, *a sixteenth-century Maya text that recalls the creation of humans.*

Maya date 4 Ajaw 8 Kumk'u—September 8, 3114 B.C.—but it was not the first to have existed. The previous world and its inhabitants were destroyed by a great flood, followed by a time of semidarkness. During that twilight time, four heroic figures emerged in the cosmos—the Hero Twins (Junajpu and Xb'alanke), their father (Jun Junajpu), and their uncle, Wuqub' Junajpu. Their adventures in Xibalba, vanquishing the evil forces that ruled the early world, were thought to prepare the way for humanity. Their story also explains the importance of the Mesoamerican ball game to the Maya culture.

The Hero Twins and the Creation of the People of the Corn

The *Popol Vuh* tells the story of two sets of twins who lived before humanity came into existence. The first twins—sons of the gods Itzamnaaj and Ix Chel—were Jun Junajpu ("One Blowgun") and Wuqub' Junajpu ("Seven Blowgun"). They were skilled ballplayers, but their loud play irritated the lords of the underworld, who invited them to Xibalba for a game. There, the lords challenged them to a series of clever tests. They failed each one and were sacrificed.

Before burying their bodies, the gods decapitated Jun Junajpu, turned his head into a gourd, and placed it in the fork of a tree. When a young maiden approached the gourd, it spat into her hand and magically made her pregnant; she then fled Xibalba to the upper world. There she gave birth to two boys, called the Hero Twins—Junajpu ("Blowgun") and Xb'alanke ("Jaguar"). When the twins were grown, their loud ball playing also irritated the gods of the underworld, and they were summoned below. Unlike their father and uncle, they won each challenge, outwitting the underworld lords and killing them. They resurrected their ancestors and returned with them to the upper world. The rebirth of their father, Jun Junajpu, transformed him into the maize god, a handsome young figure whose life, death, and rebirth was forever associated with the growth cycle of corn and a central element of worship for the Maya.

The Hero Twins' victory over the lords of Xibalba served to lessen humanity's dread of the underworld and established the necessity of making offerings to the gods to honor them. Their quest complete, the twins were taken into the sky, where one later became the sun and the other the moon.

Once the evil of the underworld was vanquished, the world experienced a time of twilight. Itzamnaaj, or First Father—the creator god, supreme deity, and inventor of writing—raised the sky above Earth and placed the World Tree at its center. He caused the sky to rotate, endowing Earth with life. Plants sprouted from the soil, including maize, which First Mother ground into meal and mixed with water to make a paste. The creator gods formed humans from the maize paste. The new Maize People, as they were called, paid homage to the gods while they waited for the first sunrise. It was a long time coming, so the humans became despondent. They wandered aimlessly in the semidarkness until the arrival of a one-legged lightning god named Tojil (sometimes called K'awiil, depicted with a serpent for one leg and a torch sticking out from his forehead).

Tojil brought fire to humans but demanded human sacrifice in return. When the dawn finally arrived, the humans burned incense in gratitude, but it was not enough. The gods made the sun so strong that everything dried out, withering the plants. Tojil again demanded blood offerings, so the early Maya offered animal blood. Still not satisfied, Tojil insisted that human blood be offered. The humans reluctantly obliged, offering a human heart. From that time forward, the Maya believed it was their duty to offer human blood to appease their gods.

Understanding the Maya Gods

Little is known about the Maya gods and goddesses because sources differ. Codices dating from before the Spanish Conquest mention 30 deities by name; however, one eighteenth-century manuscript lists 166. Part of the confusion comes from Maya gods being multifaceted, with more than one appearance, power, or name.

As with other ancient polytheistic cultures (cultures that worshipped many gods), some Maya deities had slightly different identities, depending on their powers. K'inich Ajaw was the god of the sun, kingship, war, and sacrifice, and his appearance and name in Maya art varied according to which area he was pictured as ruling. Itzamnaaj, the creator god, is always shown as an old wise man with a hooked nose and large square eyes, but he is also depicted in a different role, as Itzam Ye, the giant mythical bird sitting atop the World Tree.

Two or more Maya gods were sometimes fused, as with Tojil, the fiery god of lightning and thunder, and Chaak, the rain god, depicted in some temple images as a single being with characteristics of both gods. A particular god might be pictured as masculine or feminine, young or old, fleshed or skeletal. Each celestial god also had an underworld identity, assumed when it passed beneath Earth on its way to rebirth in the eastern sky.

Maya Codices

For centuries scholars have been poring over three surviving Maya books—the Dresden Codex, the Madrid Codex, and the Paris Codex. In 1739 the director of the Royal Library of Dresden purchased a codex from a private collector. How and when the collector obtained it is a mystery. The 74-page book, which is the most complete of the codices, contains astronomical tables dealing with the movements of the moon and the planet Venus. After its acquisition the codex became known as the Dresden Codex. The Madrid Codex, a 112-page book, was "discovered" in Madrid in 1860. It is the longest of the surviving codices, containing more than 250 almanacs. The Paris Codex first appeared in France in 1832. It is in very poor condition. The 22 pages of the codex that have survived contain prophecies and astrological information.

A fourth Maya codex, a 10-page fragment called the Codex Grolier, was reportedly found in 1965 in a dry cave in southern Chiapas, Mexico. Its hieroglyphs deal exclusively with astronomical calculations associated with Venus. Scholars believe it may be the oldest of the surviving codices.

Two pages from the Madrid Codex show the god of death heating the celestial snake to provoke rain. With 112 pages, the Madrid Codex is the longest of the four Maya codices.

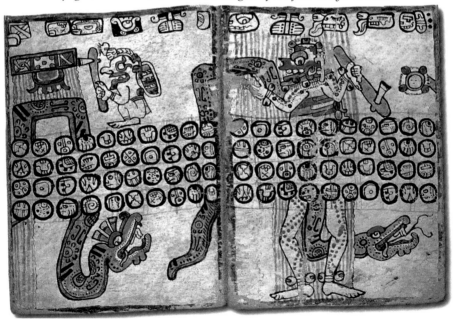

A sculpture of the Maya god K'inich Ajaw found on the wall of a pyramid. According to Maya beliefs, K'inich Ajaw was the god of the sun, kingship, war, and sacrifice, and his appearance and name in Maya art varied according to which area he was pictured as ruling.

Maya gods were sometimes depicted as infants or small children, cradled in the arms of a mortal king. This image served to reinforce the nobility's unique bond with the gods, and their vital role in nurturing those gods with blood sacrifices. Anthropology professor Karl

Taub describes the relationship depicted in such images:

> The act of blood sacrifice . . . was tantamount to nurturing the gods. The texts in the holy Maya books pair the term "suckle" with the

The Structure of the Maya Universe

Elizabeth Wagner, a scholar of Maya hieroglyphs in Bonn, Germany, points out the significant symbolism present in one particular version of the creation story: "The [re-creation] of the cosmos was achieved by setting up trees at the corners and center of the universe. The trees are associated with the colors for the cardinal points, and birds sit in them."

This imagery, of trees at the corners and at the center of the universe, is a common theme in the Maya concept of the cosmos. Murals recently discovered at San Bartolo, a Late Preclassic site in the Petén region of northern Guatemala, feature images of the five trees, each with a deity offering animal or flower sacrifices, along with their own blood. Some have nicknamed these murals—which were discovered quite by accident in 2001—"the Sistine Chapel of the early Maya" because of their age and what they reveal about ancient Maya religious thought.

Quoted in Nikolai Grube, ed., *Maya: Divine Kings of the Rain Forest*. Nordrhein-Westfalen, Germany: h.f.ullmann, 2006–2007, p. 288.

word for "embrace," recalling how, in Classic Maya scenes, the gods are held by the rulers like babies pressed against the breast. The Maya kings saw themselves as caring parents of the gods. The gods were looked after and kept alive thanks to the religious activities of the elites.[21]

The Maya Pantheon

The Maya worshipped many gods. They believed every living thing had a spirit, with a god or goddess ruling over everything in nature. Local shrines to these numerous gods were called *way-bil*, which means "place of sleep." From

time to time the gods had to be awakened and summoned to action. Despite differences between individual Maya city-states across Mesoamerica, as well as changes in beliefs and practices across the centuries of the Maya civilization, the portrayal of certain primary deities remained constant. The roles and importance of individual gods, however, varied, depending on the specific Maya dynasty worshipping them.

Several Maya gods and goddesses remained standard in appearance in images throughout the Maya region and across the centuries. The most prominent was the supreme deity, Itzamnaaj. Because of his extreme age, he was usually portrayed as an ancient figure with a wrinkled face, a hooked nose, and large square eyes resembling goggles. He was pictured wearing a headdress made of a shell that protruded from his forehead and a headband with a mirror in the shape of a flower. A pearl-studded strip emerged from the flower mirror, representing nectar or dew. The Maya associated Itzamnaaj with the morning dew and collected it each day from leaves to use as sacred water in ceremonies.

Ix Chel, "Lady Rainbow," also known as Chak Chel, was Itzamnaaj's wife and the most important Maya goddess. She ruled the night sky as goddess of the moon and water. Depicted with a wrinkled face and a long hooked nose like her husband, she was associated with weaving, medicine, and childbirth. Sometimes she was pictured as an old, fearsome goddess, with snakes for hair, jaguar claws for hands, and a skirt featuring skulls and crossbones. At other times she was a beautiful, scantily clad young goddess linked with love and fertility.

K'inich Ajaw, "Sun-faced Lord," was the sun god, one of the most powerful Maya gods. A royal figure, associated with nobles, war, and sacrifice, his worship included ritual war dances and blood sacrifice. He was pictured with beard stubble on a wrinkled face, and the Maya hieroglyph k'in—"sun"—on his body. Images of his face adorn the facades of several Classic Period temples. Each night he transformed into a jaguar to travel through Xibalba.

Chaak, the rain god, was deeply respected by Mesoamerican civilizations dating back to the Olmec and was shared by many cultures in the region. Associated with the cardinal directions, he ruled lightning, thunder, and rain. Chaak was usually represented with a long hooked nose and either an axe or a snake in his hand. Today's Maya farmers still make offerings to Chaak.

The maize god was also called Yum Kaax, or Jun Ye Nal, "First Corn Cob." His origin was linked to the resurrection of Jun Junajpu, the father of the Hero Twins. A young man with a remarkably handsome face, the top of his head was sometimes depicted as an ear of maize. According to scholar Heather McKillop, "[Jun Junajpu's] death by decapitation is a metaphor for the harvesting of corn and for death."[22] In later murals the maize god is sometimes shown as a youthful figure diving headfirst from the sky.

The primary god of death for the Maya was Yum Cimil, sometimes called Kimi. He ruled the lowest level of Xibalba. Though sometimes pictured as a fearsome skeletal god, he is also depicted as a comical, grotesque figure who has a huge protruding stomach and dances wildly. Due to the Hero Twins' victory in Xibalba, it appears that the Maya did not always look at Yum Cimil with abject fear. Sometimes they made fun of him, knowing he could be deceived with rituals and clever tricks. Unlike other gods, who had flowery breath, he spread foul smells and decay, prompting some Yucatec Maya to call him *kisin*, which literally means "the farter."

Religious Ceremonies

To keep the universe running as it should and prevent disasters or the end of the world, Maya gods had to be happy. Rituals, including blood sacrifice and vision quests, thus had to be performed on a regular schedule. When something bad happened—a drought or a flood, for example—it was the action of an angry god who felt neglected or insulted.

Religious rituals took place every day, both in peasant huts and on the steps of great stone temples. In Maya homes a mother offered bits of tortilla to Ix Chel for the health of her child. A farmer, before beginning his chores, burned incense and prayed to Chaak to bring rain to his fields. Some ceremonies involved offering food, tobacco, or alcoholic beverages to the gods. Others involved the most precious of offerings—life itself.

The sacred essence of life, called *k'uhlel*, was the blood of living things. Offering *k'uhlel* to the gods was necessary to preserve the universe. The soul inhabited the heart. Blood was the essence of the soul, making the heart the ultimate sacrifice. The type of sacrifice offered depended on the importance of the event. The offering might be small birds, animals, or human blood. Among the Maya, human sacrifice was not as common an occurrence as it was among the Aztec, but ritual bloodletting formed an integral part of religious ceremonies. Major events, such as the coronation of a new ruler, a natural disaster, a war, or the dedication of a new temple or ball court, required human sacrifice.

For years archaeologists knew the Maya offered their own blood as an offering to the gods, but they believed the Maya had not practiced human sacrifice

Creating Humans

In the beginning, before the world's creation and before the epic story of the Hero Twins, two ancient creator gods, First Mother (Ix Chel) and First Father (Itzamnaaj), created animals. They soon realized, however, that these creatures could not speak or offer prayers. The gods therefore ordained them to be servants to humans and to have their flesh eaten. The gods then tried to create humans, but their first attempts were also unsatisfactory. When they used clay, it quickly dissolved in water. They tried using wood, but that also failed. These wooden creatures looked somewhat like humans but were still unable to speak or offer prayers. According to the Maya, these creatures became monkeys. Their third attempt to create humans, using a paste made from maize, succeeded.

until late in their history—near the end of the Postclassic Period. In 1946, however, with the discovery of the Maya city of Bonampak, these theories changed. Murals and sculptures found there—dated between A.D. 600 and 800—proved the Maya, like the Aztecs, practiced human sacrifice to appease their gods. Recent discoveries and the continuing decoding of Maya hieroglyphics also reveal a higher level of blood sacrifice throughout Maya history than previously thought.

Blood Sacrifice

Individuals—both nobles and commoners—often pierced themselves with needles and stingray spines or cut themselves to provide blood for the sacrifice. Friar Landa described rituals he witnessed in the Yucatán:

> They offered sacrifices with their own blood, sometimes cutting round sections from their ears. Their scarred ears remained as a symbol. On other occasions, they pierced holes in their cheeks and lower lips and sometimes made incisions in [their genitals] or made holes in their tongues from one side to the other.[23]

Sometimes Maya priests or nobles wished to seek the gods' advice, and they entered a trancelike state to do so. Scholar Arthur Demarest describes how this was accomplished:

> Ancient shamans, priests, and rulers induced their visions with the aid of massive blood loss which naturally releases opiates in the brain. They also smoked powerful tobacco mixtures or drew upon the rain forest's natural bounty of psychotropic substances. Hallucinogens made from mushrooms were used, and perhaps extracts from morning-glories, water lilies, or the glands of reptiles.[24]

However they accomplished the trance, they believed that while in it they could directly communicate with the gods. Drugs, it is believed, were also sometimes administered to captives about to be sacrificed, especially those being prepared to be thrown into a cenote. Several accounts written by Spaniards during the Spanish Conquest tell of victims voluntarily leaping into the deep natural wells.

During the Classic Period many prisoners of war—always men—were also sacrificed. Captured kings often were decapitated. Other prisoners were stripped, bound, and paraded through the streets in humiliation. Some captives were imprisoned, tortured, and publicly humiliated for years before being sacrificed. Atop the temple pyramid, each victim was bent backward over a stone altar and was held down while a priest split open his chest and removed his beating heart. The victim's blood was burned in a vessel on the temple steps, and his body was butchered and eaten by priests and others attending the ceremony. The heads of decapitated victims were usually

This segment of a mural found at the Maya city of Bonampak shows Maya warriors presenting captives (whose heads are visible at the bottom of the image) to their king. During the Classic Period, many male prisoners of war were imprisoned, tortured, and publicly humiliated before being sacrificed.

impaled on poles in the plaza or kept in the palace as trophies and buried in the tombs of dead rulers. Captured women were sold as slaves.

Visual representations and written descriptions of Maya religious rituals tell scholars a lot about the Classic Maya, but the vast majority of sources that would explain their thoughts and beliefs have been lost to history. To learn why the Classic Period came to an abrupt end in A.D. 900, and why Maya society changed so dramatically between that date and the arrival of the Spanish in the 1500s, scientists continue to dig for answers.

Epilogue

Postclassic and Modern Maya

Many of today's Maya live as their ancestors did during the Classic Period. In rural Meso-america some Maya farmers still live in small thatched-roof houses, wear simple cotton clothes, and grow corn using tools that have changed little since the glory days of Tikal. The Yucatec Maya still call themselves the Mazehualob—"the People of the Maize"—and follow a version of the ancient 260-day Maya calendar, calling it *chol q'iij*—"Count of Days." Most of today's Maya speak a mixture of Spanish and various Mayan languages. They worship using a combination of Christianity and elements of the Maya religion of their ancestors, including a ceremony honoring Chaak, the Maya god of rain.

The causes of the ancient Maya civilization's decline have been debated for centuries. Some early scholars speculated it was caused by a sudden, cataclysmic event like an earthquake, a volcanic eruption, or a particularly destructive hurricane. But these theories have been disproved, partly because the collapse extended over two hundred years. Some suspect an epidemic similar to the Black Death in medieval Europe wiped out a large part of the population.

Some have suggested a large-scale revolt by commoners against abuses of the noble classes, an invasion, or the result of ongoing savage warfare between rival Maya city-states. Others argue that the Classic Maya overpopulated their lands, exhausted their soils, and reaped destruction because of their own short-sightedness. Today, based on scientific and historical evidence, it seems all these factors, including climate changes—specifically extreme droughts—led to their decline.

The Postclassic Period and Collapse

The final time period associated with ancient Maya studies is the Postclassic.

It extends from the collapse of the Classic Maya city-states in A.D. 900 to the arrival of the Spanish in force in 1527. Some scholars designate the last century of the Classic and the first of the Postclassic as the Terminal Classic Period (800–1000) because radical changes took place during those centuries, leading to the collapse of the cities.

Civilization during the Classic Period proved impossible to maintain in the hostile physical environment of the southern Yucatán. Scholars believe overpopulation and overuse of natural resources eventually caused the abandonment of Palenque, Tikal, Cobá, and Copán. With the abandonment of Classic Maya cities in the southern lowlands and the subsequent migration of large groups of people from those cities, populated areas in the northern Yucatán and the southern highlands gained influence. There is also ample evidence of strong political influence from civilizations in central Mexico.

Postclassic cities in the northern Yucatán lowlands, such as Uxmal, Kabáh, Labná, Chichén Itzá and Mayapán, were apparently influenced in art, architecture, and religious practices by the Toltec, a warlike culture that some scientists believe flourished in central Mexico during the tenth to twelfth centuries A.D. Postclassic Maya cities were smaller, less ornately decorated, and less skillfully constructed than Classic cities. These changes may have been due either to scarcity of food resulting from drought or as the result of political and military influence from the Toltecs. Many Postclassic cities also had defensive walls surrounding the city's center, possibly indicating constant warfare.

By the time the Spanish arrived in the 1520s, the Maya civilization had evolved into something entirely different from the Classic Period. The Maya had migrated away from their stone cities to two regions: the southern highlands of their Preclassic ancestors, and north and east to the coastal areas of the Yucatán. They remained obsessed with the calendar, worshipped many gods, and used hieroglyphics. They also established extensive sea trade routes around the Gulf of Mexico and into the Caribbean Sea.

The Conquest and Beyond

The remaining Maya kingdoms offered fierce resistance to Spain, but they were no match for Spanish firepower, nor did they have defenses against Spanish diseases. During the first ten to twenty years of Spanish occupation, hundreds of thousands of Maya died from smallpox and other diseases against which they had no natural immunity. Spanish soldiers brought southern kingdoms under their control by 1527 and northern kingdoms by 1546. Maya kingdoms in isolated forests of the central highlands held out against the Spanish until 1697. Decimated by warfare and disease, the Maya suffered more than the annihilation of much of their population. They also suffered the irreparable loss of their history at the overzealous hands of Spanish priests, who ordered their books burned, many of their idols

The ruins of the ancient Maya city of Tulum rest on the coastal cliffs of the Yucatán Peninsula and continued to be a thriving Maya city even after the Spanish arrived in the 1520s.

smashed, and forbade the use of their language.

And yet the Maya endured. They endured the collapse of their civilization and the virtual decimation of their numbers from disease. They suffered a prolonged, bloody conquest at the hands of the Spanish, refusing to submit to Spanish control until the final Maya community—Tayasal on Lake Petén Itzá in Guatemala—was conquered in 1697. They endured brutal attempts by priests to convert them to Christianity. They endured centuries of discrimination, first at the hands of Spanish colonizers, and later at the hands of descendants of those conquerors, people they called *ladinos*—Hispanic or Hispanicized individuals who moved into their territory and pushed the Maya to the fringes.

Resistance against outside attempts to destroy their culture has kept the Maya strong and has preserved their culture. In 1847 Maya peasants in the Yucatán rebelled against the high taxes and unfair land policies of newly independent Mexico in a conflict called the Caste War. For more than a year, Maya rebels fought with muskets and machetes until they had control of virtually the entire Yucatán Peninsula. Then, in 1848, on the verge of storming Mérida, the region's largest city, they faltered and were driven back into the eastern jungles.

Regrouping, some Maya established an independent nation called Noj Kaj Santa Cruz Xbalam Naj, also called Chan Santa Cruz ("Little Holy Cross"). It extended along the east coast of Yucatán, from just north of the Maya ruins of Tulum, south to the Mexico/British Honduras (now Belize) border. Partly because of extensive trade, the British government recognized Noj Kaj Santa Cruz Xbalam Naj as an independent nation. History books usually list 1901 as the date this independent Maya nation was conquered by Mexican troops, but fierce resistance actually continued into the 1940s. Today descendants of the rebels live in Quintana Roo, Mexico, and call themselves Cruzo'ob Maya. They still resist integration into the Mexican state.

The Great Terror

In the 1970s and 1980s Maya citizens of Guatemala suffered horribly at the hands of a militaristic government that seemed intent on destroying their culture. On May 29, 1978, a unit of the Guatemalan army opened fire on a group of people protesting land policies. Many of them were Maya. More than one hundred protesters were killed. Later the government instituted a resettlement policy aimed at eliminating indigenous culture, all in the name of unifying the nation under one culture and one language. According to Nikolai Grube:

The suppression of the native population in the early 1980s took on the dimensions of genocide. Union members, Catholic activists, and teachers were abducted by death squads and tortured and murdered. Maya demonstrations fell under storms of bullets, the entire male populations of villages were shot and secretly buried in mass graves, women were raped, and children were forced into military service. Maya villages disappeared from the maps, and whole tracts of land (such as the Ixil region) were depopulated. Those who had survived and not fled were forcibly resettled into so-called model villages, whose chessboard patterns of streets were watched by soldiers. The statistics convey an impression of the extent of the bloodbath and the human misery of these years, for which the Maya simply use the Spanish term *violencia*: 150,000 dead, at least 1 million refugees in their own country, and 400,000 refugees in neighboring countries, the USA, and Europe.[25]

In 1984, thanks to pressure from the world community, the Guatemalan government ceased its repressive tactics against the Maya. However, more subtle efforts continued in Guatemala and neighboring Mexico. Mayan languages were repressed as "dialects." No mention of pre–Spanish Conquest history appeared in Guatemalan or Mexican textbooks. In some cases the achievements of the Classic Maya were attributed to other cultures. The overwhelming influence of modern North American pop culture on the young also has served to further separate today's Maya from their cultural heritage.

The Maya Renaissance and the Maya Movement

Today in both Mexico and Guatemala, the Maya are making their voices heard. In 1994 a guerrilla group named the Zapatista National Liberation Army (Ejército Zapatista de Liberación Nacional, or EZLN) stormed San Cristóbal de las Casas, a large city in central Chiapas, Mexico. The group waged a largely nonviolent but armed conflict against the Mexican state. The EZLN standoff with Mexico persists today, in part because of widespread support from around the world through the Internet and other media.

Today the Maya in Guatemala, the nation with the largest Maya population, are not waging war against their government, but they have reason to hope. Elections in December 1995 brought a national government that was less anti-Maya. Under the auspices of the United Nations, investigations into human rights violations have commenced, displaced indigenous peoples

EZLN supporters protest against the Mexican government in 2001. The EZLN has been able to gain worldwide support due to the Internet and other media outlets.

are being resettled, cultural identity and human rights have been guaranteed, and Mayan languages are again being taught in schools.

Maya communities are now beginning to organize and play more prominent roles in national politics and public policy making. Maya groups in Mexico, Guatemala, and Belize are demanding the return of control over their ancestors' cities from local governments and foreign archaeologists, museums, and universities. Maya publishers are printing books and establishing Web sites in Mayan languages. Young Maya are exchanging their Spanish names for names of Maya origin.

Maya politicians—mostly women—have been elected to positions in the national government of Guatemala. Maya archaeologists and epigraphers work side by side with scientists from other countries, striving to make the history, language, and culture of their people known to the world. Maya activists are leading the way in a renewed conservation movement—one designed to preserve the natural environment and to protect their cultural heritage by creating national parks around major Late Preclassic and Classic Maya sites. The proposed Cuatro B'alam ("Four Jaguars") National Park, located in the middle of the Maya Biosphere Reserve in northern Guatemala, will be one of the world's largest economically sustainable archaeological and wildlife parks.

During her acceptance of the 1992 Nobel Peace Prize, author and indigenous rights activist Rigoberta Menchú Tum summarized the Maya worldview and their cautious optimism for the future:

We have in our mind the deepest felt demands of the entire human race, when we strive for peaceful coexistence and the preservation of the environment. The struggle we fight purifies and shapes the future. Our history is a living history, that has throbbed, withstood and survived many centuries of sacrifice. Now it comes forward again with strength. The seeds, dormant for such a long time, break out today with some uncertainty, although they germinate in a world that is at present characterized by confusion and uncertainty.[26]

Notes

Chapter One: The Rise of the Maya

1. Nikolai Grube, ed., *introduction to Maya: Divine Kings of the Rain Forest.* Nordrhein-Westfalen, Germany: h.f. ullmann, 2006–2007, p. 11.
2. Victor Wolfgang von Hagen, *Maya Explorer: John Lloyd Stephens and the Lost Cities of Central America and Yucatán.* Norman: University of Oklahoma Press, 1948, p. 75.
3. Quoted in Bruce Norman, *Footsteps: Nine Archaeological Journeys of Romance and Discovery.* Topsfield, MA: Salem House, 1988, pp. 170–71.
4. Quoted in Norman, *Footsteps,* pp. 173, 178.
5. Arthur Demarest, *Ancient Maya: The Rise and Fall of a Rainforest Civilization.* New York: Cambridge University Press, 2004, p. 114.
6. Guy Gugliotta, "The Kingmaker," *National Geographic,* August 2007, p. 76.

Chapter Two: Maya Nobility of the Classic Period

7. Simon Martin and Nikolai Grube, *Chronicle of the Maya Kings and Queens: Deciphering the Dynasties of the Ancient Maya.* London: Thames & Hudson, 2000, p. 14.
8. Nikolai Grube and Simon Martin, "The Dynastic History of the Maya," in *Maya: Divine Kings of the Rain Forest.,* p. 157.
9. Michael D. Coe, *The Maya.* 7th ed. New York: Thames & Hudson, 2005, p. 207.
10. Coe, *The Maya,* p. 207.
11. Charles Gallenkamp, *Maya: The Riddle and Rediscovery of a Lost Civilization.* New York: Viking Penguin, 1985, p. 126.

Chapter Three: Commoners of the Classic Period

12. Demarest, *Ancient Maya,* p. 116.
13. Quoted in Roger Atwood, "Maya Root: Did an Ugly, Waxy Tuber Feed a Great Civilization?" *Archaeology,* July/August 2009, p. 60.
14. Peter D. Harrison, "Maya Agriculture," in *Maya: Divine Kings of the Rain Forest,* p. 74.

Chapter Four: Greatest Achievements

15. Heather McKillop, *The Ancient Maya: New Perspectives.* New York: Norton, 2004, p. 293.
16. Michael D. Coe, *Breaking the Maya Code,* rev. ed. New York: Thames & Hudson, 1999, p. 7.
17. Quoted in *NOVA,* "Cracking the Maya Code," WGBH Educational Foundation, 2008. www.pbs.org/wgbh/nova/transcripts/3506_mayacode.html.

18. Quoted in *NOVA*, "Cracking the Maya Code."
19. Quoted in Grube, ed., *Maya*, p. 143.
20. Quoted in Grube, ed., *Maya*, p. 141.

Chapter Five: The Spirit Realm

21. Quoted in Grube, ed., *Maya*, p. 268.
22. McKillop, *The Ancient Maya*, p. 218.
23. Quoted in Grube, ed., *Maya*, p. 265.

24. Demarest, *Ancient Maya*, p. 192.

Epilogue: Postclassic and Modern Maya

25. Grube, ed., *Maya*, p. 422.
26. Quoted in NobelPrize.org, "Rigoberta Menchú Tum: The Nobel Peace Prize 1992." http://nobelprize.org/nobel_prizes/peace/laureates/1992/tum-lecture.html.

For More Information

Books

Tony Allen and Tom Lowentstein, *Gods of Sun and Sacrifice*. Amsterdam: Time-Life, 1997. This lavishly illustrated study of Aztec and Maya religious beliefs and practices includes extensive retelling of the *Popol Vuh*.

Elizabeth Baquedano and Barry Clark, *Aztec, Inca, and Maya*. New York: DK, 2005. Stunning photos, full-color art, and informative text give an overview of these three pre-Columbian civilizations.

Sheri Bell-Reholdt, *Amazing Maya Inventions You Can Build Yourself*. White River Junction, VT: Nomad, 2007. This informative book offers twenty-five hands-on projects associated with the Maya civilization. It includes projects dealing with the vigesimal numbering system, building a model pyramid, making ceremonial masks, creating a screen-fold "codex," learning to read hieroglyphs, and creating a Maya calendar wheel.

Arlette N. Braman, *The Maya: Activities and Crafts from a Mysterious Land*. Hoboken, NJ: John Wiley & Sons, 2003. This book provides activities, recipes, and crafts from the Maya civilization, along with text covering Maya history, society, and daily life. Projects include a mosaic mask, making corn cakes and chili chocolate drink, building a model pyramid, and playing Bul, a Maya children's game.

Michael D. Coe, *The Maya*. 7th ed. New York: Thames & Hudson, 2005. This complete study of the Maya is written by a leading Maya scholar. It is illustrated with color and black-and-white photography.

Laurie Colter, *Ballplayer and Bonesetter: One Hundred Ancient Aztec and Maya Jobs You Might Have Adored or Abhorred*. Toronto: Annick, 2008. Colorful cartoons humorously illustrate this guide to jobs one might have had during the Aztec and Maya civilizations, including palace jobs, food and drink jobs, military service, beauty or health careers, ballplayers, or midwives.

Nancy Day, *Your Travel Guide to the Ancient Maya Civilization*. New York: Lerner, 2000. This book takes readers back in time to the days of the Maya civilization. It tells them what they should wear, where they should go, what they should expect to eat. It covers the period from A.D. 600 to 800, during the Classic Period.

Chris Eboch, *Life Among the Maya*. Farmington Hills, MI: Lucent Books, 2005. This is a detailed, informative description of everyday life among the Maya.

Nikolai Grube, ed., *Maya: Divine Kings of the Rain Forest*. Nordrhein-Westfalen, Germany: h.f. ullmann, 2006–2007. A remarkable coffee-table book with extensively researched articles about every aspect of the Maya civilization and lavish, full-color photographs, maps, and charts. It has an extensive glossary of Maya terms, lists of major Maya sites, and world museums with Maya exhibits. This is probably the definitive source on the Maya, written by some of the best Maya scholars in the world. A must-see book!

Elizabeth Mann, *Tikal: The Center of the Maya World*. New York: Mikaya, 2002. An overview of the Maya civilization, as seen from Tikal. This book includes colorful full-page and double-page illustrations.

Lila Perl, *The Ancient Maya*. New York: Scholastic Library, 2005. This illustrated, appealing, and informative work explores Maya civilization through its social structure. Sidebars highlight archaeological discoveries, and it contains a biographical dictionary of important people and a timeline.

Robert J. Sharer, *Daily Life in Maya Civilization*. Westport, CT: Greenwood, 1996. An overview of the Maya, with a section focusing on what lessons modern societies should learn from what happened to the Maya.

Videos

The Ancient Maya: Tools of Astronomy. DVD. New York: A&E Home Video, 2006. This video offers a look at Maya astronomy and how their discoveries and techniques have influenced modern astronomy.

Apocalypto. DVD. Directed by Mel Gibson. Burbank, CA: Touchstone/Disney, 2007. Mel Gibson's movie about the Maya civilization provides excellent details about daily life in a rural Maya village, including types of clothing, food, houses, jewelry, and hairstyles. However, because the movie is set at the time of the arrival of the Spanish, certain details about the level of Maya civilization—such as city-states populated with thousands of people and priests practicing human sacrifice atop pyramids—may not be historically accurate. Nevertheless, it is a good peek into the Maya world, including the use of Yucatec Maya as the language in the movie, with English subtitles.

Mystery of the Maya. DVD. Directed by Barrie Howells. Menlo Park, CA: Razor Digital Entertainment, 1998. Originally made for IMAX theaters, this video makes the viewer feel as though he or she is actually creeping through Central American jungles before emerging to see Maya ruins.

NOVA: Cracking the Maya Code. DVD. Directed by David Lebrun. Boston: WGBH, 2008. *NOVA* tells the story of how Maya hieroglyphs were finally deciphered, with lots of background information on the Maya civilization. Available for viewing on PBS's *NOVA* Web site, www.pbs.org/wgbh/nova/mayacode.

NOVA: Lost King of the Maya. DVD. Directed by Gary Glassman. Boston: WGBH, 2007. This video is an examination of Maya murals and hieroglyphs, leading to discoveries of the tombs of Maya kings.

Palenque: Metropolis of the Maya. DVD. A&E Home Video, 2006. An in-depth look at Palenque, with background about the Maya civilization.

Web Sites

Cracking the Maya Code (www.pbs.org/wgbh/nova/mayacode/). This PBS Web site is based on *NOVA*'s video program of the same name. It features interactive pages, video clips, and lavish illustrations.

Foundation for the Advancement of Mesoamerican Studies, Inc. (www.famsi.org). An extensive Web site with up-to-the-minute information on current discoveries, excavations, and more. It also features maps, charts, and photographs of Maya sites.

Guatemala: Cradle of the Maya Civilization (www.authenticmaya.com). This site focuses on the Maya in Guatemala and has links to maps, a photo gallery, and lots of information about various aspects of Maya life, then and now.

Jaguar Sun (www.jaguar-sun.com). This is a private Web site created by Jeeni Criscenzo del Rio, the author of several books on the Maya. It features links to pages about the Maya numbering system, calendar, a retelling of the *Popol Vuh*, and excerpts from Criscenzo del Rio's novel.

Lost King of the Maya (www.pbs.org/nova/wgbh/maya/). This PBS site accompanies the *NOVA* video program of the same name. It features interactive maps, video clips, and extensive information.

Maya Rise and Fall (http://ngm/nationalgeographic.com/2007/08/maya-rise-fall/gugliotta.text). This site, which is part of the National Geographic Society, is based on a *National Geographic* article of the same name. It features links to interactive maps and a quiz on Maya knowledge.

Museum Collections

Cleveland Museum of Art. Located in Cleveland, Ohio, this museum holds one of the largest collections of Maya art in the United States, including some stelae, ceramic vessels, jade figurines, and a fine assortment of Maya shell jewelry.

Dumbarton Oaks Research Library and Collection. This museum, located in Washington, D.C., contains stone monuments, relief tablets, decorated ceramics, figurines, and jewelry made from alabaster and jade.

Field Museum of Natural History. This Chicago, Illinois, museum has a large collection of Maya ceramics and textiles from Guatemala.

Metropolitan Museum of Art. This museum, located in New York City, offers a large collection of shell and jade jewelry as well as painted and relief-ornamented ceramics, stone stelae, and wood sculpture.

Museum of Fine Arts. Located in Boston, Massachusetts, this museum boasts one of the most outstanding collections of painted Maya ceramic vessels.

Peabody Museum of American Archaeology and Ethnology. The Peabody Museum in Cambridge, Massachusetts, contains an extensive collection of Maya sculptures and ceramics.

University Museum. Located in Philadelphia, Pennsylvania, this museum holds artifacts brought back from its own expeditions of the 1930s and 1940s, including stelae, sculpture, ceramics, and jade figurines.

Index

Picture Credits

Cover Image copyright Olga Utyakova, 2009. Used under license from Shutterstock.com.
Apic/Hulton Archive/Getty Images, 72
The Art Archive/Museo Ciudad Mexico/Gianni Dagli Orti/The Picture Desk, Inc., 61
The Art Archive/National Anthropological Museum Mexico/Gianni Dagli Orti/The
   Picture Desk, Inc., 9, 73
© Stefano Bianchett/Corbis, 7
Bettman/Corbis, 7
Bernard Bisson/Sygma/Corbis, 84
Image copyright Bzzuspajk, 2010. Used under license from Shutterstock.com, 6
Sissie Brimberg/National Geographic/Getty Images, 45
Image copyright Sam Chadwick, 2010. Used under license from Shutterstock.com, 54
Martha Cooper/National Geographic/Getty Images, 21
The Creation of Man, page from "Popul Vuh" (w/c on paper), Rivera, Diego (1886-
   1957)/Museo Casa Diego Rivera (INBA), 70
© Dianni Dagli Orti/Corbis, 14
De Agostini Picture Library/De Agonstini/Getty Images, 10
© Werner Forman/Corbis, 31
Kenneth Garrett/National Geographic/Getty Images, 36
Image copyright Hannah Gieghorn, 2010. Used under license from Shutterstock.com, 62
Guanajuato, Mexico/Index/The Bridgeman Art Library, 70
© Jack Hollingsworth/Corbis, 29
© Cindy Miller Hopkins/Danita Delimont/Alamy, 42-43
Image copyright kschrei, 2010. Used under license from Shutterstock.com, 17
© Otto Lang/Corbis, 24
© Charles and Josie Lenars/Corbis, 28, 56
Image copyright rj lerich, 2010. Used under license from Shutterstock.com, 19
© Craig Lowell/Corbis, 53, 68
Model of a ballgame (pottery), Mayan/Worcester Art Museum, Massachusetts, USA/The
   Bridgeman Art Library, 65
© Francis G. Mayer/Corbis, 6,
Joyce Naltchayan/AFP/Getty Images, 7
Image copyright Pierdelune, 2010. Used under license from Shutterstock.com, 58
© Carl & Ann Purcell/Corbis, 82
Image copyright Qing Ding, 2010. Used under license from Shutterstock.com, 13
Terry W. Rutledge/National Geographic/Getty Images, 34, 39, 48
SEF/Art Resource, NY, 78
Time Life Pictures/NASA/JPL/Time Life Pictures/Getty Images, 64

About the Author

Charles and Linda George have been writing children's nonfiction books for more than ten years. They have nearly sixty books in print on a wide variety of subjects—from ancient civilizations to world religions, from the Holocaust to civil rights and black nationalism, from working dogs to the world's pyramids. The Georges were both teachers in Texas schools before "retiring" to write. They live in a small town in western Texas.